To my children:
I am incredibly proud and honored to be called your mama!
I love you more than words!

CONTENTS

CONTENTS

ACKNOWLEDGEMENTS

To my Lord and Savior, my everything, thank you for sharing your story in my life. At times I would not have said that, but I would do it again if it meant that one more soul would be saved. Thank you for blessing me in the utmost of ways and for holding on to me. Thank you for never letting go of me, even if at times I didn't want to hold on to You. Thank you for all the blessings you so freely give to a sinner like me.

To my wonderful and amazing children, may the Lord present this book to you at the right time in your life. May you never forget the hardships that this life will inevitably bring, but use this book as a reminder of the faithfulness and peace that God has and will provide; the peace that you can always rest in. Seek and follow Him alone.

To dad: you have made me the proudest daughter by allowing me to walk alongside you through your deepest time of need and by allowing me to be a part of the story of your salvation. To my mom, who I am watching grow in the love that Christ will always show her, I thank you for all you have done for me.

To my husband who always encouraged me that I was good enough to write this book when I didn't have the confidence to even start, who always encourages me to follow through with all the dreams that I have wanted to accomplish, thank you for sharing your story even if you weren't keen on doing so, God knows it will be an influence and bless many people. Thank you for being my best friend.

To Mark Mingle and the entire team at Trilogy Christian Publishing. I cannot express my gratitude for what you have done for me. I never imagined that the words written in this book would be something I could share with the world, but you have made it a reality.

To Kristy: your generosity and enthusiasm for this book gave me the courage to continue to make my dreams become a reality! You have blessed me in incredible ways by pre-editing this book, helping to make it the best it can be. You have a brilliant way with words! I am beyond grateful for your friendship.

To Jaime: your growing friendship has been a blessing to me and my family's life. Thank you for sharing your wisdom to bring truth to life through this book. Thank you for honoring God in your teaching!

To Inspired and Enchanted Photography: my dear friends Naomi and Nikki, you have been there since the beginning watching my family grow through your lens. Thank you for sharing your incredible talent through the photos that will last a lifetime! Love to you both!

To Marti Evans, author of *Wilderness Wanderings: Devotions from the Desert*. Your kindness, guidance, and prayer gave me encouragement and hope that I could bravely follow the plans that I felt the Lord calling me to. Thank you for sharing your insight in "what's next." Thank you for welcoming me in with open arms, even though we had never met or spoken before. You showed me Christ's love and I hope to pass that on to the next generation of dreamers.

To you who have taken a chance and picked up this book. May it bless you in exceptional ways and give you hope that you are never alone in your journey. May it show you that in the darkest of trials you can be wrapped in His perfect peace!

"Jesus looked at them and said, 'With man this is impossible, but with God all things are possible.'"
Matthew 19:26 (NIV)

PROLOGUE

We all have those defining moments in our life. These moments, whether joyous or disheartening, shape the very essence of the questions we all face: "Why God?" "What's next?" and "Where are You?" We wonder, "Where can I find that peace beyond understanding that everyone talks about?" and "Is that even something that's able to be found?"

We ask God why He allows us to walk through storms. We blame Him, even though He isn't the one who caused our sin. We ask God where He is and why He hasn't shown up yet to save the day. We contemplate and question the very goodness and existence of our Great God. We want to follow Christ and all that He stands for, yet we want to walk the easy life when trouble ensues. In the midst of anxiety, depression, loneliness, and worthlessness, we are quick to fall into Satan's pit of despair.

We wonder why we can't seemingly "find" the peace that surpasses all understanding when we only need to look up to God and "see" it. We wonder why God doesn't bring comfort in our troubled times because comfort will surely bring peace, right? We want the instant gratification that comes with saying, "I trust you Lord" and "I have faith in you God," and God grants our requests, even though we often think we have "earned" them; meanwhile we try to control every outcome of every one of life's scenarios behind the scenes.

I know because I have been there. I have been to the darkest depths of that pit, asking the same questions, wandering around trying to make sense of how I got to this new and unfamiliar place.

That pit taught me that, in this world, we can choose life or death. If we choose to fall deeper into Satan's trap, and believe the lies that he so cleverly uses to target our deepest insecurities, we choose death. But if we choose to cling to the only One who can change the course of our hearts and lives in an instant, we choose life. When we choose life, we tap into some of the most amazing aspects of who God is and how He will provide every time. We can be wrapped in the peace and comfort that only God can give when all seems lost. This may likely come in ways we never had in mind or ever wanted.

For me and my family, when all seemed too far gone, God showed up in miraculous ways and wrapped us in His perfect peace.

It was April 9, 2015. My husband and I woke up to a day like any other. I got ready to head off to my job and my husband went off to his, roughly around the same time, about six in the morning. I worked in food safety at a local industry, which meant I worked on the factory floor. Due to safety and sanitation requirements, I was not able to carry my personal mobile device. Instead, I was issued a company cell phone, only accessible by my superiors and the other plant employees. Unless someone official was in need, it was extremely hard to get in contact with me during my workday for personal reasons.

I was often very busy at the start of the day, with a variety of pressing tasks. That morning, when I finally had a second to breathe, I checked my work cell to see what was next on my agenda. I discovered a missed call from our security department, not all that unusual in my position. I assumed an auditor had arrived to inspect our facility. When I returned the call, the gentleman who answered informed me that I needed to call the police department right away for a reason that had nothing to do with quality control.

I'm sure everyone has thought about *that* phone call. You know the one. The one that could come to you as easily as it could anyone else, but you never really believe it will. The call that may come to a friend, a neighbor, or a co-worker, but certainly one that could never come to you. We whisper in hushed circles about those calls that have changed others' lives in an instant, all the while hoping that we never have to face the tearing down of our own comfortable walls of protection.

However, *that* call was my reality, at eight o'clock in the morning on a typical day, much like any other.

As I hurried to my desk to phone the police department, I was met by my boss, Elise, at the top of the stairway. The look on her face was tell-tale. The situation was serious.

Now Elise is one of the most amazing people I have ever met. Her drive to get the best out of people was unlike any other. She molded those in whom she saw potential and I admired her qualities and character. When I looked at my boss, I saw my future self. She is what some might describe as a firecracker; demanding of respect, but like a mama bear, ready to protect her cubs.

As I looked into her stricken face at that moment, I felt strangely like one of those bear cubs. With measured calm, she proceeded to inform me that I needed to get to the

Hershey Medical Center right away as my husband had been in a severe car accident. From what she could gather, he was unresponsive at the scene. With gentle urgency, she gave me the final pronouncement—she would accompany me to the hospital and that, if we didn't hurry, I might be too late.

My head began to spin. My thoughts ran to the present, to the immediate, to panic. With increasing dread, I worried about how my mortal life might change forever. Little did I know at the time, but God's thoughts were well ahead of me and focused much more on the immortal.

What I didn't know that day, was that my life and relationship with Christ was about to change forever. I can still remember every feeling I went through from the minute I found out about the accident. My thoughts buzzed on the traffic-filled drive to the hospital, while I sat in the Emergency Room waiting area, while I wept with my boss (who consequently took the lead and carried me through, in typical mama bear style).

I have never felt so much and questioned so much all at one time. I began with, *"WHY? God, Why?"* From there, I dissolved into thoughts of the irony of the date and the timing, *"Why on this day, the day of our four-year wedding anniversary, Lord? Why, when I am four months pregnant with our first child?"*

I continued to spiral. I wavered from the throes of desperate panic to outright anger. *"How could YOU do this to me, Lord? Haven't I always been a good and faithful servant? What have I done to make YOU so angry with me? Am I being punished?"*

You see, when life falls to pieces—when everything you thought you had control over slips out of your fingers like dust falling back to the earth—anxiety, fear, and depression can quickly take hold. What infects the mind can quickly affect the heart and soul. Doubt of God's goodness, and quite frankly His existence at all, can creep in while lies start to take hold of your every emotion.

None of this is inherently wrong in the moment. We are human, after all, and subject to emotion. However, staying in this state is not what God intends for us. What He does intend is for us to turn to the Savior who bears the burden of all worries, fears, and struggles. And that, my friends, is what I eventually did.

I'll admit that it took some time, but I eventually took all of that junk to my Father in Heaven and laid it at His feet. And in that moment of prayer, as I cried out to the Lord—at some points for what I wasn't even sure—the winds seemed to change in an instant. I felt an overwhelming calm and peace wash over me. I knew, that while things were about to get very tough, and with my husband's life hanging in the balance, all would be okay.

We would be okay.

I would be okay.

Not by my own hand. Everything was out of my control, but God was *in* control.

"What if shattering (of our lives) is the only way to get dust back to its basic form so that something new can be made?"[1]

What if all the pain and suffering that we go through, all the breaking, is the only way for God to take us back to our original form in which He created us? What if that is the only way for God to transform us into someone new—someone we were always meant to be, but couldn't see for ourselves, a new creation?

This is not a book of groundbreaking theological principles, but a story. The story of an ordinary, 27-year-old girl who knew nothing of God, being molded into a daughter of the Most High by the experiences that God allowed, the love that He has shown, and the peace that He has brought.

Dear ones, this is for you; for those of you who struggle with depression, wondering when the darkness will finally turn to light. This story is for you who get anxious, falling faster and faster, trying to grab hold of anything to make it stop.

This is for those of you who feel worthless in this very broken world, trying to find your identity in the first thing that passes your way; for you who are looking for God's modern-day miracles.

This story is also meant for those of you who need proof that through all your darkness God's goodness can still shine upon you and His peace can still be wrapped around you.

This is for you.

My prayer is that this book would be a light guiding you up out of the darkness into His loving arms, and that His words would be a beacon of hope, illuminating the fact that you are never alone.

"Have I not commanded you? Be strong and courageous. Do not be afraid; do not be discouraged, *for the Lord your God will be with you wherever you go*" (Joshua 1:9, NIV).

With much love,
Lindsey Krug

"For this is what the Sovereign Lord says: I myself will search for my sheep and look after them. As a shepherd looks after his scattered flock when he is with them, so will I look after my sheep. I will rescue them from all the places where they were scattered on a day of clouds and darkness. I will bring them out from the nations and gather them from the countries, and I will bring them into their own land. I will pasture them on the mountains of Israel, in the ravines and in all the settlements in the land."
Ezekiel 34:11-13 (NIV)

Chapter 1

THE EARLY YEARS

Picture this: a young girl who loves sweatpants, sports, no make-up, and a ponytail being ridiculed by her "friends" for the way that she looks. This young girl wants to fit in so badly that she asks one of them to help her pick out some new clothes. She wants to be fashionable. She wants to fit in.

Her friend graciously agrees and picks out the most amazing pair of jeans to go with a blouse—totally outside the girl's comfort zone. The girl, nonetheless, is desperate for acceptance and willing to give it a whirl.

When school comes around on Monday, she proudly dons the new garments, sure that her "friends" will now approve of and accept her. Now, imagine her shock and embarrassment as she enters school to meet with the faces of laughing onlookers—among them, the very "friend" who was responsible for selecting the outfit.

Imagine the damage done to the young girl's heart as a result of this incident, during some of her most socially precarious and formative years. Imagine the image that will come to her mind every time she hears mention of the word "friends."

Unfortunately, the incident was not an isolated one when it came to this girl's interaction with others. I invite you to continue to imagine this same shy freshman, who wants to fulfill latent dreams of participating in high school choir. She learns that she must undergo a tryout but knows that she'll be grappling with genuine stage fright. She's assured that it's merely a formality, so she decides to persevere. She musters all of her courage and sings her heart out. The new teacher is glib. The girl is patently informed she doesn't have a powerful enough voice to continue. When she inquires further, it is explained to her in simpler terms. She is not allowed to join. The girl is so devastated that she walks away from music altogether and buries her passion for singing deep down inside of her, vowing never to return to it.

Imagine that same girl—in high school now, as she vies for her parent's attention. She tries so desperately to earn their love by working hard to place third in her graduating class. She excels at all sports. She knows they will love her accomplishments, even if they can't love her as Christ designed.

This girl draws the conclusion that there is something flawed within her, so the harder she works to add external achievements, the less those flaws will matter. Her wins and triumphs will give her the gifts of likability, status, and value.

She doesn't dare step out of line or get into trouble for the fear that her parents would stop noting her "unblemished record" and would ultimately stop loving her.

She looks for worth in the world around her, completely unaware that there is another path, until one day when she is introduced to the ultimate path—a life walking with Christ.

On shaky legs as a new believer in Christ, she begins to try to come to terms with what salvation means; the end to her dependence on the world's opinions to give her value. It seems a breath of fresh air, a true transformation of thought and belief, but it is not without its fledgling issues.

Imagine as she walks boldly into her family as the first person to proclaim the gospel, only to be told that she is nothing more than a hypocrite. She is shaken to her core, but she prays for faith to continue on this newfound journey, despite her rejection.

Imagine her as a first-time girlfriend, entering into her boyfriend's family. With no example from her own home life, she does not know how to function within a healthy spiritual environment. And even though she is about to walk into one of the closest-knit circles of believers she has ever known, as a new believer, she's initially intimidated to meet them. Will they accept her? Will they need some "help" to accept her in the form of her achievements?

Picture her missing the mark and trying for years to do everything she can to earn their love and respect, instead of simply being herself. Imagine as she tries to convince them that she is worthy of being a part of their tight-knit family, only to have them reveal their unconditional love for her. As a result, she prays for God to fill her with the worth that He's intended for her to have, and to remind her of the worth that she doesn't have to earn.

Imagine her, the college athlete who gets bullied by the older players because she is confident in her ability, only to find that her hard work is blasted as being a "kiss-up" tactic. Other voices tell her over and over again that she will never be better than those older athletes, that she will never amount to anything.

Although she's made great gains with the steadfast example of her boyfriend's family, the girl still feels so worthless that she is on the edge of walking away from all the hard work she has dedicated to the sport that she loves. She wrestles with God about how and why she should love those who would never love her, the ones who continually mar her self-image.

Imagine her as a college graduate, venturing out into the unknown world and landing a job at a Fortune 500 company. She walks into this dream job hoping to use all that she has been taught to climb the ladder of success, regardless of the male-dominated company culture. Her fledging confidence is dealt a hefty blow when she gets passed up for an accolade against two males, without any explanation as to why, even after she was told that she would receive it. Her lingering sense of inferiority grows. Despite her progress, she still forgets sometimes. She fails to see herself as a beautiful woman, made in the image of God.

Imagine the new mother who wants so desperately to have a special bond and relationship with her daughter. She puts pressure on herself to try to create a "perfect" relationship—unlike anything experienced in her family before. She idealizes it to the point that when those fantasy thoughts don't measure up to the real, broken world, she crumbles at the painful disappointment. As a result, she believes that she is not good enough even to be a mother and she allows Satan control of her mind, instead of letting the God of peace fill her with hope. She prays God will remind her that even though she is not a perfect mother, she is perfectly paired to be this little one's mama.

Imagine the stay-at-home mother whose family doesn't understand her choice to leave the wealth and status of her job to stay home with kids. She builds identity in her kids and allows the love that they show her to fuel her motivations. She prays for confidence in the woman and mother that God has called her to be.

What do all these stories have in common?

They are all mine.

They are painfully hard to write.

They are authentically real.

They are precisely the feelings I have held for most of my life.

They reveal the failures of man in this sin-filled world.

Some are lies that have impacted and shaped my life from a young age, some are triumphs found only from the grace of our precious Savior as He has stayed by my side during my ongoing spiritual growth.

Some of those negative experiences built insecurities, some unearthed insecurities I didn't even realize existed. Many I stuffed so deep down, that I became numb to their destructive power. I began to identify them as "normal."

I've since learned that these are false identity markers in the pathway of my life; they're Satan's beckoning road signs, drawing me down the forbidden, dark path.

When I was younger, I didn't even know that God could and does speak to His children. I have spent most of my life caring way too much about what other people think of me and listening to their voices and my own more than God's. The problem with these negative voices is that we often keep listening, hoping that some encouragement will slip in even if by mistake. We forget the source of voices cannot compete with the source of our true identities.

While the majority of these stories are seemingly negative, they are the stories that chiseled and scraped away at the clay God was molding. They show what and who I believed that my identity came from, they show where I thought love came from. They show a broken-minded, naive young girl—a girl who didn't grow up in a family who went to church every Sunday or knew all about the love that came from Christ. They show a girl who allowed the words of others to define her; a girl who didn't know that she was a daughter of the King, beautiful in every way because she was made in God's image.

But within these stories are also the stories of hope; hope that no matter what evil was trying to do in my life, God was holding onto me. He was walking with me through my trials in order that I might get to the place where I am at now with Him, just as He was walking with His disciples in Mark, Chapter 6. In this chapter, Jesus asks His disciples to go out in a boat on the lake ahead of Him. As Jesus sees the wind pick up and the disciples straining at their oars, He walks out on the water toward them (Mark 6).

Paul Tripp explains that Jesus was not interested in halting the difficulty, He was interested in the people in that difficult situation. "God will take you where you have NOT intended to go in order to produce in us what we couldn't achieve on our own."[2] If Jesus didn't care about us and the circumstances of our lives, He wouldn't have made the walk.

The Concept of Generational Sin

The evil one has very cunning ways of tricking us into believing that we are safe from harm and free to live OUR own lives. One of those ways is through generational sin. This term is not my trademark, but a concept that I have seen play out in the lineage of my family.

In *The Screwtape Letters* by C.S. Lewis, we see Screwtape, a high-ranking servant in Satan's army, writing to his nephew Wormwood (a demon) on this very matter of keeping the next generation in the dark about the previous generation so as to not allow them to realize that change needs to take place. Screwtape writes, "Since we cannot deceive the whole human race all the time, it is most important thus to cut every generation off from all others; for where learning makes a free commerce between the ages there is always the danger that the characteristic errors of one may be corrected by the characteristic truths of another."[3]

We see the pattern of generational sin, even in the lives of some of the most beloved members of the Bible. When Abraham was staying in Gerar he told Abimelek, king of Gerar, that his wife Sarah was his sister and Abimelek took Sarah not knowing that she was really Abraham's wife. Abraham told this lie because he believed that Abimelek would kill him (Genesis 20).

Later Abraham's son, Isaac, proclaims the same lie as his father to the same king. Isaac went to Abimelek, king of the Philistines in Gerar, because there was a famine in the land. When men asked Isaac about his wife, Isaac replied that she was his sister because he believed that the men would kill him (Genesis 26).

We see the concept of generational sin in the Israelites when they do not remember what God has done for their ancestors. They make the same distrustful and disobedient choices toward God that their ancestors did. The Lord raises up Moses in Pharaoh's own house after all the Hebrew babies were to be killed. He leads Moses back to Egypt after he had run away to deliver the Hebrew nation out of bondage from the hands of the Egyptians. God, through Moses, parts the Red Sea and allows all the Hebrews to walk across on dry land, crushing their enemies in the raging waters behind them (Exodus 14).

After all that the people of Israel groan and complain that they are wandering through the desert. The Lord provides manna from the heavens and water when the people need it, and the people still wish that they would have died back in Egypt. They further forget all that the Lord had just done for them (Exodus 16, 17).

The Lord gave them the Ten Commandments and while the Lord was presenting them to Moses on Mount Sinai, in their impatience, the Israelites made their own idol and began to worship a false god (Exodus 19-32). Because of their disobedience, that particular generation was not allowed to enter the promised land and were forced to wander through the wilderness. As the next generation rose up, they were afraid at first to trust God and His plans for them to take over Jericho and finally enter the promised land (Joshua). As their distrust and disobedience in God grew, the Israelites asked God for judges and kings to rule over them, enslaving them as they had been in the generation before.

We see it in the kings of old as the next generation's king was sometimes worse than their father, or mother. "Ahaziah son of Ahab became king of Israel in Samaria in the seventeenth year of Jehoshaphat king of Judah, and he reigned over Israel two years. He did evil in the eyes of the Lord, *because he followed the ways of his father and mother and of Jeroboam son of Nebat,* who caused Israel to sin. He served and worshiped Baal and aroused the anger of the Lord, the God of Israel, *just as his father had done*" (1 Kings 22:51-53, NIV).

Generational sin has plagued families for decades. Sadly, most individuals ensnared in this type of sin pattern, do not understand the basis of this very dangerous concept. Without the knowledge of salvation, false concepts of living creep in, from broken relationships, to emotional turmoil, to faith in self-driven works as a way to be "good enough" to earn a trip to Heaven. All are based in false concepts—lies from below—and things that have been practiced from one generation make their way to the next.

My family was no different. I learned that signs of affection were for the weak and deep conversation was best kept for the theologians. I began to struggle with these false concepts when I realized that I was beginning to emulate the patterns of generations that came before me. Patterns that were outside of God's design.

Broken family dynamics, crippling anxiety about abnormalities, death, and the afterlife, and holding onto true feelings never fully revealing what was underneath the facade; these are a few patterns that I carried on. No-one in my family had a personal, deep-rooted relationship with God, so these concepts became my normal reaction to outside stressors.

I grew up in a small town just outside of Hershey, PA, the daughter to two blue-collar workers. My father was raised in the Catholic Church, but he never went to church or practiced religion after he became an adult. My mother had attended a church as a young person, but from my view, had developed a very cynical view of church, people who went to church, and faith in general. I remember hearing the words *hypocrite* and *church* being used in the same sentence frequently.

My childhood is one of a mystery to me. It is not talked about much, I don't remember a lot, and there are little to no pictures to document those life moments. This is the same as my parent's childhood, complete anonymity. It is never talked about from any family members, no stories told, no family videos shared. I know little to nothing about what my parents were like as kids.

From all perspectives on my part we just existed. I had no real purpose to my life, no direction, no guidance. I was a lost soul, and I didn't even understand what that meant. Most of my younger days I felt unfavored and overshadowed by my older brother who took most of my parent's attention with the choices that he made in his life. And there was no way that I could talk to either of my parents, especially about deep issues, so I held in any emotion, questions, and thoughts, bursting in my mind to find answers.

The one thing that made the most sense in my life, however, was sports. The portal to all my happiness and worth. I knew who I was when I stepped onto the field. I had confidence. I had power. I controlled the game, the outcome, my future. Sports became an idol for me. So much so, that every weekend I would play at a higher level hoping to achieve a worldly congratulations and praise for my performance.

Sports gave me recognition at school and acceptance with other students. Sports was a way to connect to my parents. I played the sport they loved, after all—softball—so I knew the harder I worked the more attention I would receive. My dad would spend night and day practicing with me, totally devoted to making me better and pushing me in every way. Softball fueled my parents. They began to live their dreams through me vicariously and it became their idol as much as it was mine.

When it came to softball, my parents didn't miss anything. They were on the sidelines at every tournament on the east coast and throughout my entire career. Even in college, they never missed a single game. While I admire this most about them, it also reinforced the dangerous idea that I had to keep performing to keep them glued to their seats.

I didn't dare give up or quit. I could never face disappointing them in this area, it was too important to them. I never really asked myself if a hectic college sports assignment was what I really wanted. I loved the game more than anything, but my sole identity was tied to keeping my parents happy and attentive at the next game. I never considered the day when softball would end.

I never ventured out to explore other skills, interests, or possibilities for my life. When I went to college, I had no idea what I wanted to study, I went for the sole purpose of playing softball and earning the worth I so desperately sought. Somebody saw that I had skill and pushed hard for me to attend their school and play for their team. They wanted me. That made me feel worthy. So, I went, and I played. I never consulted God. I never prayed about what and where God wanted to send me. I chose a path that I wanted to take, and, in my ignorance, God never even factored into the equation.

As the end of my softball career loomed, a feeling began to grow in my heart. Much like a gentle tugging, it felt like there was something else out there that I needed, something more than sports and seeking.

From a young age I'd always had an interest in the church. I remember going to a small church in Bellegrove, PA with one of my best friends and her family. I participated in the Christmas program, attended VBS (Vacation Bible

School) in the summer, and on occasion would go on the summer retreat. As I got older and life got more complicated, I would occasionally attend a different church with a different friend until one day there were too many things competing for my affection, and I left the church altogether. Sundays were not a day for the Lord in my family anyway, so it wasn't really a big deal to me. If anything, by keeping this interest under wraps, I was better off because I wasn't looked at as the outcast of my family. But, as I faced the end of my softball career, this feeling of being pulled in another direction never left me. I had a yearning in my heart to find out what it was.

As I began to ponder this hidden yearning, I began to gain some perspective. What I can say about perspective is that it is monumental. While it can't change what has happened to us in the past, it can change everything about the outcome if we allow God to shape it. Perspective can help shift my attitude from looking at myself, to looking at God. The perspective that I had as a child was blurred by my inward struggle with my selfish attitude and desperate need for acceptance. My perspective was filled with lies that I wasn't enough for anyone. My attitude was warped by the evil that I couldn't see circling around me, but God wasn't done shaping that perspective—and that is my everlasting encouragement.

"The longer I live the more I realize the impact of attitude on life. Attitude is more important than facts. It is more important than the past, the failures, than successes, than what other people think or say or do. It is more important than appearance, giftedness, or skill. It will make or break a company...a church...a home. The remarkable thing, however, is that every day we can choose the attitude we will exhibit for that day. We cannot change the inevitable. The only thing we can do is play on the one string we have and that is our attitude. I am convinced that life is 10% what happens to me and 90% how I react to it. And so, it is with you and me…we are in charge of our attitude. Just one more thing… Attitude is doing what is right when nobody is watching."[4]

It is amazing how our minds latch onto the negative in our past experiences and bring them to the forefront first. We tend to block out the positive and push them deep within our memory banks so that they are the first to be discarded. However, what we may believe to be negative and attach a traumatic experience to may in-fact be a positive in God's eyes.

What is our definition of negative and positive anyway?

For me the positive was the easy, fun, wealthy, comfortable, stress free, selfish way. The negative was the messy, hard, unstable, painful, hurtful way. But my life would look very different if I was always living in "my" positive. My life is better now than it has ever been and to the world the last five years have probably looked mostly negative. It's about perspective. Are we viewing the world through our lenses or that of Christ's? Are we turning those moments of darkness thrown our way into moments of light, glorifying the Lord? Are we praying for God to take away the pain in the moment, the hurt of the situation, or are we praying for a new perspective, a better attitude, an opportunity to be blessed in ways that cannot come when life is peachy? An opportunity to bless those around us. An opportunity to save a life.

My parents loved me very much, but in a very worldly way. To no fault of their own they couldn't love unconditionally because they didn't know how to be loved unconditionally. The love of Christ didn't fill their hearts waiting to be sprinkled on those around them or poured into the next generation.

I share this to show where we came from. What we grew up understanding. Where we believed our value, worth, and identity was wrapped in. I share this to show you the weaknesses of our earthly bodies, the lies that Satan would use over and over again in the course of the generations of our lives.

These patterns meant that I took every word man said about me or to me to heart, a personal jab at my entire existence. I was a total people pleaser. I cared too much what others thought of me and the impact that they had on my life. I feared man and not God and Satan knew this, used it, and relished in it. These insecurities would crop up in pivotal moments throughout my life. These thoughts and beliefs that I had about myself led me down a certain path of life.

I love the quote Stasi Eldredge uses in her book, *Becoming Myself*, about the way and the truths we think and believe about ourselves; "Watch your thoughts for they become words. Watch your words for they become actions. Watch you actions for they become habits. Watch your habits, for they become your character. And watch your character, for it becomes your destiny! What we think, we become."[5]

In Priscilla Shirer's study *Armor of God*, she talks about how Satan plays on our weaknesses. "The evil temptations that appeal to your specific desires are not accidental. The discord and disharmony that threaten your most valuable relationships are not coincidental. The temptations that tug at you during your weakest moments are not uncalculated. None of these things are happenstance. They are his deceptive tactics (and that of his evil entourage), specifically designed and personalized to keep you from experiencing abundant life... Satan knows that he cannot destroy you. The best he can do is to make your time on earth futile and unproductive, to suffocate you with sin, insecurity, fear, and discouragement until you are unable to live freely and fully. He can't "unseat" you, but he can intimidate you and render you ineffective and paralyzed."[6]

This was my emotional and spiritual foundation.

My shaky, unstable foundation.

These moments, designed by Satan to steal joy from my life and keep me from living the life God fully intended for me to live, were used by God to build strength in me, character, courage. The platform for a strong, brave, firm foundation, which I would need, for all that we would walk through in the coming years and for the rest of my life!

Wrapped Up

*This book is my deeply personal story, so I wanted to give you additional resources to connect the key content to your life. At the end of each chapter will be a section called "Wrapped Up" with additional resources, mainly questions to reflect upon; all in hopes that these items will open up your heart, bring a light to dark places, and draw you closer to God!

Reflection Questions:

- Are there lies that have shaped your life from a young age? What voice speaks the loudest in your life?

- Are there areas of your life that the enemy has targeted or frequently attacked (i.e. self-confidence, self-image, identity, faith in Christ?) Is there a pattern or progression to these attacks?

- Have you witnessed generational sin in the history of your family? If so, how could God be calling you to break this cycle?

- How do you determine if an experience is positive or negative?

- Do you feel God asking you to change your perspective on a particular situation in your life?

"Do not be anxious about anything, but in every situation, by prayer and petition, with thanksgiving, present your requests to God. And the peace of God, which transcends all understanding, will guard your hearts and your minds in Christ Jesus."
Philippians 4:6-7 (NIV)

Chapter 2

THE TURNING POINT

On the drive to the hospital, I prayed. Sitting in the ER waiting room and then the ICU waiting room, I prayed. For three hours, from the time I found out about the accident until the time a doctor came to tell me if my husband was alive or dead, I prayed, but not in the way you might think.

I prayed in anger to the Lord. I was wholeheartedly angry at the Lord for allowing this tragedy to happen on this day. I was angry that on this day—the day that was to commemorate walking down the aisle to marry my best friend, I might become a widow. On top of that, I prayed in anger, outraged at the possibility that the child I was carrying would never get to meet his or her daddy.

I was angry that, even though I was surrounded by friends and family, I felt so terribly alone. I was angry that it was my husband and not me. He was the one so deeply rooted in Christ, he was the one that led me to the Savior, he was the one who did so much good for others. Why was it *him*?

Then, as all of the anger lashed around inside of me, I began to break. The emotions bubbled up and flooded my soul. The anger gave way to desperation. I was angry with the Lord, but I needed Him urgently. I began to pray differently; only slightly at first, but then in raging torrents. I prayed for courage to step into this new sea of unknown activities and emotions that were sure to come. I prayed for just one last look into my husband's eyes, to tell him that I so deeply loved him. I prayed for a miracle. And as I prayed, I felt something I have never felt before—something beyond all human explanation. I began to feel an overwhelming peace.

It was not to last, however.

I had yet to find out the status of my husband's life—would he survive the injuries he sustained in the accident? I was sure that the medical personnel were busy giving him the best and most urgent care that he needed, but I so desperately yearned to know if he would live.

In the interim, desperate in that waiting room, I did not get that answer. What I did get was a call from the police officer in charge of the investigation. He asked me if I had made it to my husband in time. I had no answer to give him.

He asked me if I would like to have the details of the accident. Unsure, I consented. The police officer proceeded to tell me that my husband was hit on the passenger side door. He used the term "T-boned" by a semi-truck carrying roughly 80,000 pounds of limestone. Apparently, the truck driver was cruising at about 55 mph when he ran a red light. As a result, the truck pushed my husband's car into a curb, and then a telephone pole before it finally landed on its side in a tree.

I literally could make no response. It was if I knew my husband's fate the moment the officer stopped talking. To this day, I do not even remember the end of that call.

This second shock left me numb. People around me were talking, but it was as if I was hearing muffled voices speaking in foreign languages.

My brother-in-law, Josh, was sitting next to me at the time, and he was just what the Lord knew I needed. He was the first one to arrive at the hospital, mere seconds after me and he just sat there, holding me, not saying a word. He prayed with me and sat with me. He wrapped me up in his strong, comforting arms the way I imagined God would hold on to me if He'd been sitting next to me.

Shortly after, a chaplain from the hospital arrived and asked if he could pray for me or call another pastor that I knew to come help us through. In all honesty, I should have been happy to see him, but inside I thought all of this was too much to handle. I knew that God wouldn't give me more than I could bear, right?

I was four months pregnant with our first child. Inwardly, I wondered how much the instant stress, anxiety, and worry would affect the baby. I worried that it might even lead to a miscarriage. I was already working about fifty hours a week at my job, now this. I thought, *Even if my husband lives, will he be a vegetable that needs my constant attention?* Tears began to stream afresh. *Will he remember who I am, who he is, that he is about to become a dad?* Another angry prayer escaped me, *"God I am NOT strong enough to handle this!"*

Little did I know, in my anger, I'd spoken some of God's truth. I wasn't strong enough on my own. God was about to walk me through devastation to miraculousness, but He wasn't about to let me go it alone.

At that instant, dissolving into my grief, I felt someone pick me up and hold me tight. I was devastated, but for the second time that day, I felt an overwhelming presence touch my soul. My only explanation is that the Holy Spirit had surrounded me. He wrapped me up tight in His peace—the peace that surpasses all understanding. I felt it, right there in that ICU waiting room of the Hershey Medical Center, just as I felt my brother-in-law's arms around me.

When the doctor finally came out nearly three hours after the initial accident, he started with one phrase, "Your husband is alive. It's bad, but he is ALIVE!"

The doctor proceeded to tell me all of my husband's injuries, and what the next steps would be, but I didn't care. No matter what happened in the coming days, weeks, months, my husband was *alive*, and I had the renewed hope that I would get to look into his eyes and talk to him once more.

When the doctor was finished giving me the status update, he said that I would be able to go back and see my husband after they finished stabilizing him. He was very careful to warn me that Ben was in pretty bad physical shape and that he would probably look nothing like the guy I'd known. The doctor also informed me that my husband didn't quite understand what was happening to him, so it was imperative that I try to remain calm throughout my interaction with him. He explained that, due to the severity of his injuries, my husband would need to be physically restrained for a while so that he would not awaken and attempt to remove any of the tubes or instruments. This was also to avoid him harming himself, in the event of him being disoriented.

I took a deep breath. This was my husband, my Ben. If the doctor needed me to be calm, then calm I would be. I understood that he may look a little battered, but none of that mattered to me. I wanted to see him so badly. I wanted to comfort not only him, but myself. I wanted to see with my own eyes that he was really, truly alive.

As I finally was able to enter his room, my heart sank to the pit of my stomach. If I thought the police officer and the doctor had prepared me, it was apparent now that I had grossly underestimated even their most careful of pronouncements.

I had never seen anything like this; truthfully, I wasn't nearly as ready as I thought I was to walk into the room and see what lay before me. There were about a dozen tubes and wires hooked up to monitors, Ben's face was ripped up and broken, his head actually had staples in it, and he was hand-cuffed to the bed. Instant tears sprang to my eyes. What was I going to do next?

My brother-in-law, Andrew, describes the first time seeing his brother as one of the hardest moments to live through:

> *I entered the room. It was one room, amidst a whole floor of emergency rooms. Life and death hung in the balance for many people here. As I stepped in, my eyes immediately went to my brother. But my eyes couldn't just take him in, they were filled with wires, braces, stitches, staples…the blood, the swelling, the bruising, the brokenness. I'd only ever seen a human being lying like this on TV or in the movies. My sweet brother was broken beyond any belief. He was still alive yet distorted in ways I couldn't imagine. Ben's head was swollen immensely, and his right eye protruded like a black softball.*

It just hung there, seemingly lifeless. Out of sheer instinct, I worried that the brace around his neck looked like it was choking him, due to the edema of his face. I literally couldn't believe my eyes. How could this be my brother?

Now that I was fully in the room, I took in my surroundings. Lindsey and my other brother, Josh, were there. I went to them. We embraced and talked. I don't remember many specific moments during this time. I do remember Lindsey sitting at one point, tear stains on her cheeks and a blank expression on her face.

What she needed was for us to just be there. The surreal horror of those moments wasn't for talking, but just for being. Thankfully, Josh gave her that. I admire him for his whole posture during this event. It left a deep impression on me.

One thing I do remember very vividly is Ben trying to get up. It happened within the first ten minutes or so of my being there. This moment was one of the worst moments of my life. Even thinking of it now makes me deeply distressed. Just moments before he started to stir, he seemed almost lifeless on the bed, and now he was moving, turning, trying to get up.

I wish I could describe accurately why this memory makes me feel so upset. I just remember that his movements were so robotic looking as he navigated the neck brace and wires. The doctors had told us about the massive amounts of sedative they had given him, but his body was fighting, it was stirring, trying to cope with the trauma it had endured. As Ben's body spun, he looked like Frankenstein arising from a mighty slab. This swollen, battered, bloodied brother of mine was rising, which was the last thing I had expected him to do. The worst part was the look he gave us. Contrasted next to his black swollen droopy eye, his good eye, when it opened, looked even more deranged. It opened so wide, and was so full of terror, I almost got sick on the spot. Let me assure you that this is not an exaggeration. I will never forget the look of panic he gave us. His eye registered a terrified, confused shock. The worst part of it was, I couldn't help him. The doctors came and got him settled down again, but the whole moment, which lasted only seconds, was horrifying. I hope I never have a moment like that again.

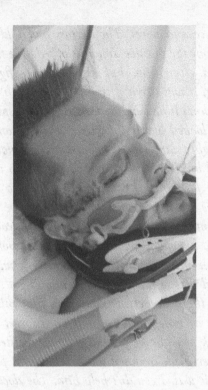

As I look back now, it is difficult to read these words of description, especially when I think that they were written as both Ben's family and I grieved for the love of my life, my dearest husband. The realities of that day were like none other than an arrow piercing my heart!

How I remained calm and collected is a miracle to me, but not in its origin. I felt weak—I wanted someone to take care of both me and my unborn baby. I didn't feel strong enough to endure not only my present circumstances, but all that was to come.

But God knew exactly what I needed, and when I needed it. He knew that my relationship with Him was not as stable as it could be, so He allowed me to learn what it looks like to be deeply rooted in Christ.

I didn't grow up with that knowledge. When I became a believer, I had a very skewed view—when you accept Christ, you were "saved." Therefore, you were good to go, forever. I didn't know it then, but I was soon to find out that the surface level understanding of salvation is not all that God intends. I was about to learn that He doesn't just want us to say yes to Him, He wants our everything! He wants our hearts, our souls, our minds. He wants us to wake up every morning with Him on our minds and go to bed singing His praises for another day of life.

As I sat there, I began to think. There was much fretful, idle time in those first days, yet God wasted none of it with me. I began to ponder deeply. My expectation was for God to show up and erase my hurt, set things back to normal, to wave a wand and wake me up from the terrible nightmare. Instead, He gave me deep inklings that I would carry with me from that place—seeds that would slowly grow in the soil of my heart.

Reluctant and untimely as it felt, I began to realize that perhaps I'd inserted my husband, Ben, in God's place more times than not. Ben was the one that I woke up thinking about, the one whose praises I sang, the one I lifted high. Ben was the one who I looked to when trouble arose or when I needed help. Ben was the one who held me together. Now, Ben was not even able to talk to me. He didn't even know where he was or what had happened, and there was no way he could help me through this situation.

I wondered. I dared to consider. Could a good God allow a tragedy to happen in order to teach us something? Could a good God allow us to walk through trials not because we did something wrong or for our punishment, but to change our perspective? Could a good God use this tragedy with Ben to help me grow closer to Christ in ways that couldn't possibly be achieved when things were going smoothly in my life?

> "Consider it pure joy, my brothers and sisters, whenever you face trials of many kinds, because you know that the testing of your faith produces perseverance. Let perseverance finish its work so that you may be mature and complete, not lacking anything."
>
> James 1:2-4 (NIV)

> "Therefore, since we have been justified through faith, we have peace with God through our Lord Jesus Christ, through whom we have gained access by faith into this grace in which we now stand. And we boast in the hope of the glory of God. Not only so, *but we also glory in our sufferings, because we know that suffering produces perseverance; perseverance, character; and character, hope.* And hope does not put us to shame, because God's love has been poured out into our hearts through the Holy Spirit, who has been given to us."
>
> Romans 5:1-5 (NIV)

A very long time after the events of Ben's accident, I grew to learn that God wants our every thought and action to reflect that of Jesus. We will falter, He knows that, but He wants us to recognize that and acknowledge those sins and lay them at His feet. I wanted the simple and easy version of the Christian life. The one where I accept the Lord as my personal Savior, then close the book, His final work completed simply in me and without any mess. But a true Christian life will be an endless novel of twists and turns, with pages of unpredictability where God is the main character, and we are merely supporting roles in His grand bestseller.

In the years following the accident, God would show me that there is so much more as we grow closer to Christ and tap into and have power that only He can give. He would also show me that growing closer also comes with a high price, and that it places a veritable target on your back for evil to hunt. You see, Satan hates when we grow closer to Christ. He is more than happy for us to accept the Lord, like I did, taking the passive Christian existence and living out our days devoid of the power of sanctification. If we don't know who God is and what His truths are by reading the Bible and crying out to Him, then in our deepest time of need we can be easily tricked into believing this lie. We can also be tricked into thinking that we know more than God or talked into believing lies about our circumstances and our character, pulled down a path that we never imagined we would be on. Ultimately, we run the risk of being tricked into believing we are nothing and that evil has and will win.

At one point, I sat next to Ben holding his hand as he lay mending from the inside out, I noticed there was a bag of his personal items sitting on the windowsill of his room. I started to look through it to find a bag of bloody clothes, his wallet, and his wedding ring. His wedding ring. The reminder to me in that moment that the day of the accident had been our four-year wedding anniversary. At that time four years ago, I'd been getting my hair and makeup done and preparing to walk down the aisle to meet this man, the one now lying broken on the bed beside me. I turned that wedding ring over and over in my hand asking God to perform a miracle and allow us to spend many more anniversaries together and I slipped the ring on my finger.

Each doctor that came into the room told me something new about Ben's condition. He had suffered multiple broken ribs, a broken collarbone and sternum, multiple fractures in his skull including a section that had broken in two places and pushed his skull into his brain, damaging the brain and causing bleeding, and eventual death, to that particular part of his brain tissue. He also had a broken ear drum, an enormous gash on the top of his head that they had to staple shut on scene to get it to stop bleeding, and a broken eye socket. Unfortunately, the bone pinched the optic nerve of his right eye, rendering him permanently blind on that side.

Struggling to absorb all of the information that they were giving me, I remember the thing that fascinated me the most was the minor details about all the major issues. These minor details were used by God to save Ben's life, these minor details, had they been worse, could have ended his life in an instant. The fracture in his skull actually helped to relieve the brain pressure when his brain started to swell from all the trauma. The fact that it was also running vertically through the ear (instead of horizontally), meant that he was able to live. We were later told that, had it been horizontal at that particular location, it would likely have killed him.

Ben also scored a "seven" on the traumatic brain injury scale (eight or less on the scale is classified as a severe traumatic brain injury). This meant that the part of his brain that had died could lead to memory loss and a loss of his personality. Yet, during his fleeting moments of coherence, it seemed that his memory and personality were very much alive. God had His hand in the details. We could see it; we could feel it.

When Ben finally opened his eyes, he struggled to get out of bed. His unknowing desire was to get up and move around, to rip all the cords and tubes from his mouth and body. It was painful to watch him struggle knowing I couldn't do anything to help him, knowing that the restraint was for his own good, and viewing the confused look in his eyes. They seemed to plead—*why aren't you helping?*

Eventually, one of the doctors asked him if he knew who I was. We were astonished when he responded with my name, Lindsey. It felt like a weight lifted off my shoulders—not only was he alive, but at least for the moment, he knew my name!

Miraculously, as we continued to ask him questions about life, he continued to answer them correctly. Slowly, he started talking more and even making jokes. We knew that deep down inside this broken body was Ben—the Ben that we all knew. The Ben that we all loved. The doctors couldn't believe what they were seeing, and we felt we were witnessing a true miracle.

Nearing the end of the first day, I hadn't eaten much, I was still in my work clothes, and I was exhausted. As I left Ben's ICU room for the first time in hours, I was met with a swarm of friends and family—Ben's family that had come in from out of town, friends that live near and far, my maid of honor all the way from Philadelphia, several pastors from our church, an old boss that just stopped by to see if I was okay. These people showed up spilling God's love all over that hospital. The first thing they asked was if we could pray. And as one body, huddled together, we prayed. For those who didn't believe in that room, we prayed.

Prayer is powerful! Never underestimate it! Prayer taps into the communication chain to our Mighty God! I had never prayed as though I had a right to pray and ask God for anything before. I had never prayed with a heart that truly believed God could answer those prayers. I had never prayed with confidence or prayed for the BIG things in life. Why do we act as though we have no authority to be authentic with God? He already knows what we need and what we are going to ask for or not ask for. I learned that prayer is a catapult shooting boulders straight through the heart of evil! Priscilla Shirer, in her *Armor of God* study, talks about prayer in this manner, "Prayer is the mechanism that brings down the power of heaven into your experience. It is the divinely authorized method that activates your spiritual armor and makes it effective. Prayer alerts the enemy to your awareness of his intentions while safeguarding you from attacks. It is his (Satan's) kryptonite. It is what weakens and unravels all his ploys against you."[7]

> "Then they cried out to the Lord in their
> trouble, and He brought them out of
> their distress. He stilled the storm to a
> whisper; the waves of the sea were hushed.
> They were glad when it grew calm, and
> He guided them to their desired haven.
> Let them give thanks to the Lord for His
> unfailing love and His wonderful deeds
> for mankind."
>
> Psalms 107:28-31 (NIV)

"For the Spirit God gave us does not make us timid, but gives us power, love and self-discipline."

2 Timothy 1:7 (NIV)

"So do not fear, for I am with you; do not be dismayed, for I am your God. I will strengthen you and help you; I will uphold you with my righteous right hand."

Isaiah 41:10 (NIV)

"God is our refuge and strength, an ever-present help in trouble. Therefore we will not fear, though the earth give way and the mountains fall into the heart of the sea, though its waters roar and foam and the mountains quake with their surging."

Psalms 46:1-3 (NIV)

The right people at the right time

The ICU nurses at the Hershey Medical Center were AMAZING; I couldn't have more positive things to say about their professionalism and hard work. We were not technically allowed to have more than one person with Ben at a time because of the severity of the injuries, but they often allowed two, so that someone could be with me for support while I was with Ben.

During the next few hours of that first day, it seemed that there were hundreds of doctors and residents who came in and out of his room. Ben had a specialty doctor for almost every part of his body—eye, ear, head, chest. With each attending physician came a dozen or so students, as Hershey is a teaching hospital.

All of Ben's doctors were extremely knowledgeable, patient, understanding, and comforting. They were able to provide me with as much information as they could in those early hours and days, but they did so with grace and kindness.

As a special thank you for all the physicians had done for my family my boss, Elise, brought them a goody basket of assorted chocolates. With her initiation of appreciation, she brought a light not typically shown in the darkness of this unit, one in which death and life most regularly hung in the balance. As a result of this gesture, it opened up an opportunity for us to talk openly with many more staff members than anticipated about God. We were even able to proclaim the good news of Jesus Christ when they made observations about the miraculous situation and our reaction to it all.

You see, God often sends people into our lives that we need at just the right moment in ways that we don't expect or understand and in turn, we may become the very people they need as well. Ben could have been taken to another hospital that was much closer, but due to the severity of his injuries the EMTs drove right past that first hospital. In the moment I didn't understand why they would risk losing Ben by driving past a perfectly adequate hospital, it didn't make sense, and I did not understand how trauma care worked. But I couldn't see the big picture that God had in store for us.

One person God clearly placed into our situation was a young ICU nurse. The one that God specifically placed in that role during our time of need. This young man brought us all much comfort. He was knowledgeable in his field and gracious in the Lord. This nurse made a particularly important impression on my father-in-law, Dan Krug. Dan has this to say about him:

> *God goes with us through the dark times of life and oftentimes, He uses His people to journey with us and to help ease our pain. Such was the case in our terrible moment. He struck me as very compassionate and very knowledgeable. As I talked with our nurse and asked him questions about Ben's condition and treatment, I learned that he was a believer in Jesus and that he attended the Hershey Area Evangelical Free Church. God comforted me by having a brother in Christ care for my son. I was grateful that Ben was being cared for by someone who was very capable of attending to Ben's physical needs while also having some understanding of my spiritual turmoil. It meant a great deal to me to have someone praying for Ben as he was treating Ben. Our nurse also encouraged me when he told me that many doctors and nurses were on hand to receive Ben and were waiting for him when he arrived at the hospital. An entire trauma team was assembled to give Ben the best care that was available. I remember thinking how grateful I was that Ben was placed where he was.*

Ben was placed exactly where God wanted him to be.

He was placed with the exact people God knew we needed—those who would be an encouragement to us all and would push to strengthen not only Ben's physical body but our spiritual "bodies" as well.

My father-in-law gives another account of that Godly push:

> Two days after the accident, I experienced something that I will never forget. I figured that Ben's condition would force him to be bed-ridden for many days. To my surprise, this particular ICU nurse had Ben out of bed and walking the hallway with his help and the use of a walker. I couldn't believe it! Here was Ben, unconscious the day before, with a fractured skull, broken ribs, a severe concussion and an injury to his right eye. He'd been initially thought dead at the scene by the paramedics, and here he was walking the hospital floor. It was as if God raised him from the dead. It was at this point that I felt that God truly spared his life. I didn't know how severe his injuries would be and I didn't know all the ramifications of his accident, or what was to come for that matter, but I did come to a point where I felt that he was going to survive and God comforted my heart. Light pierced my darkness.

After two days, Ben was moved from the ICU to the main hospital. During this time, two major things took place. One is a story from a man that God sent to watch over Ben right after the accident and the other is a story of the courage that God gives in our most fearful times of need.

I had just left Ben's hospital room to grab some dinner with my parents when he showed up. A stranger to us. The man told us that he was the one who saw exactly what had happened at the scene of the accident, how, for him, it was just like watching a movie scene unfold before his eyes. As he sat at the intersection waiting for the light to turn green, he saw a semi-truck barrel into the side of Ben's car. This man described the scene in detail. He'd had his window down and heard a slight screech of tires. He instinctively hit his breaks, noting that he'd just narrowly escaped the same fate as Ben. He speculated that, with the rate at which the truck was approaching, any impact to his driver's door would likely have resulted in his own immediate death. Instead, he watched as Ben's car was pushed right in front of his and all the way into a tree.

The man testified that he jumped out of his vehicle immediately after the impact and ran right over to Ben's car. He found Ben, unconscious. Since the car was turned on its side, there was no way to get Ben out. Instead, the man just held Ben's hand and waited with him. He called the police and kept telling Ben to hang on—to hang on until help arrived, to hang on just a little longer. The man was visibly disturbed and heartbroken at the retelling of his story. I can't imagine what he must have experienced, or what he saw when he came upon Ben's mangled car. I would get a glimpse into those horrors a few days later when I was told that I had to pick through the car and get all our personal belongings out of it in order for the car to be released from the impound.

The insurance company began to call. They needed me to go through the car so they could release it from the impound. My first thought was that I did not want to have any physical images in my mind of what the scene of the accident looked like. I didn't even want to drive through that same intersection in the future. How was I going to do this—pregnant and alone? I reluctantly accepted help from my mom and dad, mostly because I knew my dad would be able to bust through the wreckage to pull out any of Ben's personal items.

As I walked up to the car, I was instantly sickened by what lay before me—basically a pile of scrap metal all twisted together. Thankfulness welled up in me that no-one was in the passenger seat, as that part of the car was completely non-existent. And the blood—it was simply everywhere! I could see every broken bone, bruise, gash, and wound that my husband had mapped out on the car, an utterly horrifying scene. The car told every moment of the story. My heart lurched. How had Ben survived all of this?

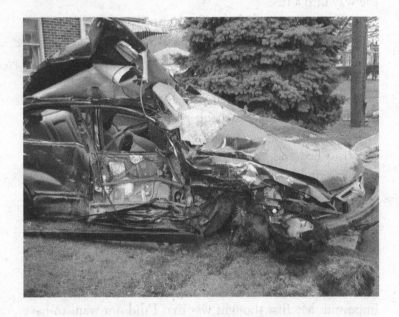

But then, at that extremely tense moment, I felt a prodding. There had been light at the end of that dark tunnel. I turned to look at the driver's seat, perfectly encapsulated by God's grace. While the car was shoved together, caved in on itself, and in every way mangled, the driver's seat and steering wheel were virtually untouched. I could almost see God wrapping His arms around my husband and taking the blow for him. In that instant, in that place, I thought to myself—isn't that exactly what Christ does for us every day? He takes on the sins of all. He wraps us up and protects us from others and ourselves. He holds our life in His hands. Ben could have, and from the worldly perspective, should have died that day. But he didn't. God saved him for something greater. We wouldn't see what that something was until further down the road, but God could see it. God could see that there was still work to be done.

The next few days and weeks of our lives were a blur of visiting Ben in the hospital, still working about fifty hours from either my home or the office, taking Ben to the myriad of doctor appointments, physical therapy, speech therapy, and occupational therapy. After about five days the doctors told me that they were going to send Ben home with me. Send him home with me after a week? He was doing well, but not well enough to go home with a pregnant wife who knows nothing about the around-the-clock medical care he would require. His brain was stable at the moment but could start to swell if a problem arose. I instantly began to worry—what if it was a problem that I may never notice? He needed medication and therapy to get back onto his feet. He needed to learn different skills and conditions that his body would now wrestle with. He needed to be watched over every second of the day, and he was not yet able to be left alone. He needed time to adjust and heal both physically and emotionally and I had no idea how I could possibly give all of that to him.

After pleading with the doctors to find another solution, God provided one like a spring in the desert. One of Ben's doctors was able to get Ben a spot at a new and specialized brain trauma rehabilitation unit. It was a unit designed for Ben's specific condition, one with no stimulation and twenty-four-hour-a-day care. It was an extension of care that would allow Ben's body the peace and stillness to fully heal as much as God would allow.

We learned that Ben, however, would never be the same. It would take years to understand the full extent of his brain trauma. It would take years to understand the personality changes. It would take years to grieve the loss of the man I married and realize that I now had a new husband, one that I didn't choose. I worried about how it felt regarding the adjustment. He lived, yes, and I should be thankful. But he wasn't the same husband, father, or person that I once knew and was excited to grow with. I had a new husband, and it would take years to navigate this terrain. Terrain with no road map that I am still working my way through today.

This accident was a turning point in my relationship with Christ, it had to be. I thought that I was living for Christ when I accepted Him. That was a lie. I was still living for myself. I had never experienced anything like this before and with its magnitude I had nowhere else to turn. This accident brought me to my knees in prayer, brought me to the word with an open heart, a child-like faith. I had a hunger for God. My faith was tested and made stronger. I was humbled by the realization that I have no control over my life and learned to put my wholehearted trust in God's hands.

My relationship with Christ became real. Not just a picture of someone that I read about or hear about at church. A living, breathing, friend. One that I can talk to and go to just as I am, free of shame, guilt, and judgment. But as I took what the Lord was showing me and tried to move forward with my life all that I had learned would soon be lost.

The Israelites were taken out of slavery and bondage and brought forth to a promised land. God provided everything that they needed when they needed it, even in the midst of their complaining. He made them His chosen people, but they abandoned God and made the same mistakes over and over again. And God tried to warn them over and over again. Like the Israelites, I would make the same mistakes and fail to put my full trust in God when the "next big thing" came.

I was not prepared for what was about to happen next. As Priscilla Shirer said in her *2019 Going Beyond Simulcast*, "You are either going into a storm, in the midst of a storm, or coming out of a storm."[8] After finally coming out of one storm I was about to head into another one, one that almost took my life.

Wrapped Up

Reflection Questions:

- How do you react when God's plans conflict with your desires?

- Have you counted the cost of following Christ?

- Like Ben's preserved driver's seat, have you experienced God's protection? If so, do you often remember that time with a thankful heart for God's faithfulness or do you try to forget the pain?

- Are there areas in your life you are unwilling to surrender to God?

- Does God allow us to go through pain to accomplish a greater good?

"As long as you are proud you cannot know God."
—*Mere Christianity*, C.S. Lewis

Chapter 3

FROM THE OTHER SIDE

I magine waking up in the hospital and not being able to recall how you got there, what day or month it is, or why you were strapped to the hospital bed unable to move while you watched your loved ones doing nothing to help you. Would you be scared? Would fear run through the course of your blood, flooding into your heart? What if you saw things that you couldn't explain? Would you believe that you were in Heaven? Would you be angry? Would peace about the situation be the first thing you feel? I cannot answer these questions, but my husband Ben can surely paint a picture of what this looks like. He was willing to share his experiences that he wrestled with through the hardships, disappointments, and suffering God allowed him to endure:

My memories of the days I spent in the hospital after the accident have been a challenge to reconstruct. While I spent several weeks in the hospital and rehab, I cannot decide if it felt more like only a few hours or months. I remember little of the dozens of doctor appointments and endless scans and tests I endured or the daily grind of requiring assistance to do basic functions like eating, dressing, and showering. Based on these recollections, I would be tempted to think I was in and out of the hospital in a day or two.

Digging a bit deeper into my mind I find another layer. The memories here are numerous, filled with very raw emotion and pain. This is the part of my journey that I had to endure without anyone except God; my internal quest to uncover the truth of my situation and my subsequent battle with myself over how I would react to what I found. I have spent a significant amount of time trying to convince myself that these memories are dreams, a product of my traumatic brain injury, or simply unreliable. My goal is not to attempt to convince you of their validity, I cannot do that. I can tell you that after going through a time of severely doubting them, the Lord very clearly convicted me. He reminded me of His unceasing presence and friends, I have never doubted since.

It all began so quickly, perhaps since I cannot remember anything from four days prior to the accident. Four days before the accident was Easter; I can vaguely remember our church's service but that is it. The next thing I know I am jerking awake in a hospital bed. Confusion, disorientation, disbelief, fear; each jostling to choke out the other emotions. Looking around I see Lindsey and my two brothers in the room with me. But something is wrong with them. For some reason they are unmoving, frozen. Assuming something is wrong with Lindsey or the baby I focus on her, asking her if she is alright and if there is a problem with the baby. When no one responds I begin to panic, this is also the moment that anger settled into my heart and took root.

I began shouting as loudly as I could, saying anything I could think of to try and get their attention. When I finally stopped screaming at them, I started crying. Fear like I had never experienced before settled over me like a heavy quilt. Shutting my eyes, I shouted at God, "Why is this happening?!" After a moment, I opened my eyes to see that things had changed. My vantage point was now different. I was looking down upon myself in a bed surrounded by my family in a hospital room. It felt like I had been plunged into an ice bath, I had difficulty catching my breath, and besides being utterly bewildered, was now in total panic. Grappling for something, anything, to hold on to I turned my head and noticed something even more strange, trees.

I turned cautiously and found I was in the woods. A warm, soft, but bright sun shone overhead through the canopy. All thought of the hospital room melted away as I took in my surroundings and realized I was standing on a path. I still felt fear and anger as I looked around, but they were muted, distant. The woods and path felt familiar, reminding me of a path I had walked hundreds of times as a kid. As I made this connection I remembered, *if this is the path that I think it is then there should be some metal chairs to my left.* I turned slightly and yes, there were the gray metal chairs that our neighbors had put there for some reason. But hold on, someone was sitting in one of them.

For a long while, I just stood there looking from the man in the chair, to the woods, and back again. Neither of us spoke for some time, I really had no perception of time at this point. Without looking at me he smiled and said, "Well Ben, what do you want to do?" I asked what he meant. "Do you want to go with me or go back?"

As the words came gently to me, I felt the weight of that question like a lead blanket. In that moment I was aware that something very serious had happened to me and that I was being presented with a very real choice. I was also able to finally think with some clarity. I thought about my life and without hesitation I said, "I'm not ready to go with you. I am going to fight and do whatever I need to do to get back to them," pointing back to the hospital room. Then he looked at me for the first time and I was sure I knew him though I did not know how or from where. As I returned his gaze, I felt something dissolve over me, strength, hope, peace. I was also beginning to feel another sensation, pain. It began as a dull pressure in my head, but it was increasing steadily. As the pain grew the man, chairs, and woods began to melt into a haze and were replaced by the scene from the hospital room that I had previously occupied. Except this time, it was different. The people were moving, they were alive, they were real, and the pain consumed my mind.

Through the myriad of exams, tests, scans, and conversations with doctors I learned that I had been T-boned by a tractor trailer, who ran a red light, while on my way to work, the day of my anniversary, no less. This had resulted in broken ribs, several fractures in my skull, swelling of my brain and subsequently a massive concussion. I had a severely swollen right eye, and I was very excited for that swelling to subside so I could finally see correctly. The most frightening diagnosis I received was when I was told that part of my brain had filled with blood and was "dead," or essentially non-functioning. What a weird thing to think about, part of my brain is dead. While that is difficult to process, I cannot express how blessed I am. There are any number of disabilities or abnormalities that I could have as a result of this injury. However, none of my motor skills were affected and I have been told that most people cannot even tell that I have sustained serious injuries. To me that is absolutely incredible, and I cannot see how anyone can attribute this to luck. What a blessing our "near misses" or "I should have died" experiences are, they should point us directly to God and His providence.

Next came possibly the hardest day of my life. I was in an office with Lindsey taking a vision test. I could only read the first line or two with my left eye but considering my glasses were off that was no surprise. The doctor told me next, he was going to cover my left eye and I was to repeat the test. But rather than cover my left eye he put his hands over both of my eyes. For a second, I thought, *he's playing "guess who" with me*. I thought, *Okay, I'll play along*, even though I thought it was really strange. He said, "Go ahead Ben." *Alright well since he is messing with me, I will mess with him*, I thought. I opened my left eye and noticed that he was doing a poor job covering that eye, so I was able to use this eye to see some of the letters. Plus, I thought I remembered them from just looking at the chart. I had used this trick before, remember some of the letters to improve my results and avoid glasses as a kid. The doctor was pleased and took a step back. I looked over at Lindsey who eyed me curiously and said, "Wait a minute. Ben, were you looking at that with your left eye?" I was incredulous. How could my own wife call me on this in front of the doctor. I was caught so I admitted that I had. The doctor stepped forward and tried the test again, this time he made sure to cover my left eye. But he was again covering both eyes. "Okay Ben, let's try this again." Now very agitated at everyone in the room, I responded, "You have to move your hand away from my right eye, how do you expect me to see it?"

Lindsey responded, "Ben his hand is not in front of your right eye." Now I was about to lose it on her. I quickly put my hand up to my right eye and confirmed, she was right. There was nothing obstructing my eye. I was thoroughly confused. How could this be and what did it mean? Someone muttered something along the lines of "this is what we feared." Without really understanding my predicament, I had that punch in the gut feeling. On top of all that I was dealing with, now something else was wrong. The doctor explained to me that one of the fractures in my head ran behind my right eye socket. When this happened, my optic nerve was pinched and consequently damaged. Until now the doctors were not sure of the extent of the damage because, while there was still blood flow to that eye, it had been swollen shut. The amount of swelling, I am sure, is why I had not come to this realization on my own. Due to the nerve damage they feared my eye would not work properly, if at all.

They were right, it hit me so hard and so quickly it took my breath away.

I...am...blind!

Defeat became a new friend. I felt defeated in every way.

The tidal wave of emotions that crashed over me was overwhelming. I was angry, jaded, broken, beaten, resentful, humiliated.

I was so angry that this had happened to me. I hated the person that did this to me. I hated myself for letting it happen. I hated God for not protecting me.

I wanted to kill something with my bare hands.

I wanted to take a baseball bat and smash everything I could find.

I wanted to punch Jesus in the face.

I was completely broken.

I was utterly defeated.

I regretted my choice in the woods.

A few nights later I awoke and found that I was in something like a courtroom and the man from the woods was in the stand. He was not looking at me or saying anything, his eyes slowly shifted from somewhere in the distance down to his feet and back. I was not going to miss this opportunity. Standing up I took aim and began firing accusations and threats toward him.

"You say that you are always with me!"

"You say that you will be my shield!"

"You say that you will work all things to the good of those who love you!"

"You say that you are the Great Physician!"

"I say...bull!"

My anger boiled over and before I knew what was happening, I was shouting and trying to invent new ways to tell him how much I hated him and wanted nothing to do with him. Clearly, if he had been honest with me and told me what going back would cost, then I never would have gone. Breathing heavily, I stopped my tirade to catch my breath. After a few minutes of silence, he looked at me. I expected my feelings to be echoed in him, I anticipated a retort. But in his eyes, I found nothing of what I felt in my own heart. I found absolutely no anger. I found understanding. This man understood me completely, fully, thoroughly. Yet, I did not feel shamed, despite all the filth that I knew was present in my heart and mind. I felt as if he truly knew me and I felt acceptance. This unexpected grace disarmed me.

As I looked away from the stand, I saw for the first time that someone was sitting across from me at the table I stood behind. This was not just anyone, it was me. I studied myself and was sure that I was looking into a mirror. Before I could consider this, I heard myself from across the table say that I was doing well. I looked back at the stand, the man was still looking at me. With our eyes locked I whispered one phrase, *"Help me."* Then, I felt the clarity that I had back in the woods. It was as if I was seeing clearly for the first time since this debacle began. I was struck by a thought, *This cannot go on. This is going to destroy me. This anger needs to be dealt with.*

I had known that my present course was unsustainable. All that I wanted to do was "get back" at a few people; the man who hit me and God. Then it hit me like a wave of freezing cold water—I needed to be free from this yoke, I needed to forgive. Looking at myself I said, "I know what I need to do." The other self answered, "Surely you cannot mean that. You cannot let them off the hook, you cannot let them win. You owe it to yourself to hold this against them or else they win. We both know you do not want them to win." I took a deep breath and looked at myself. In that other face I saw all the anger and resentment that had held me captive just moments ago and I responded, "I know, but I cannot do this anymore. I am done. I have seen that there is nothing here but pain and death. The only one I really hate is you."

I heard myself start arguing about why I was wrong, why I should know that I need to hold those responsible to account for what happened to me. I closed my eyes and the anger flared back, but this time it was different, it was directed at a very specific target, the person sitting across from me. I shouted, "This can't go on!" Then I leapt across the table onto myself and began fighting with my bare hands. We grappled and rolled across the floor. Then everything changed.

Opening my eyes, I discovered that I was in a new room, my rehabilitation had begun. Waking this morning was different. While physically I was still in severe pain, I knew that something had changed. I had changed. I was no longer angry or wallowing in defeat. It felt like being rescued or set free from oppression. Before today I had been unable to cast aside any of my emotions that had done nothing but choke me. Now I could breathe and not be poisoned by the flares of resentment that sprang up at the physical pain caused by breathing deeply. Something had been done to me that I was unable and unwilling to do for myself. It was as if once I began fighting against the horde of sinful, selfish thoughts and feelings in my heart, no matter how meager my strength, a force other than myself routed my enemy.

It seems so simple to write but in actuality it was monumental, like the joy of a first breath after being held under water. After days of stewing in my own anger and self-pity I had finally decided enough was enough. Holding on to anger and bitterness did not provide one ounce of relief, instead it was poisoning me. It took time for me to understand this and when I finally did, I did not have to rely on my own strength as I had feared. Jesus, in His great mercy, was with me when the battle began, He was just waiting for me to fire the first arrow. This morning marked the beginning of my spiritual recovery.

There were still many questions that had not been answered, first and foremost in my mind was simply, "why?" Why did God allow this to happen to me? In His grace God led me to the following passage that I believe partially answers that question.

John 9:1-3 (ESV)

> "As He passed by, He saw a man blind
> from birth. And His disciples asked
> him, 'Rabbi, who sinned, this man or
> his parents, that he was born blind?'
> Jesus answered, 'It was not that this man
> sinned, or his parents, but that the works
> of God might be displayed in him.'"

Think about the cost to this blind man. We probably cannot imagine the difficulties of being completely blind in this part of human history. He would have had to rely on others to meet his basic needs; food, water, shelter. Did he deserve this? Jesus said that it was not for anything that he or his parents had done. This had a profound impact on me. Whether I deserved what had happened to me or not is beside the point. God being glorified is of greater value than the years the man had spent blind. In no way does this minimize the sacrifice this man made, but it should help us to see the immense importance and worthiness of God's glory. Thinking about the man's situation in terms of fairness would be a great mistake. It seems to me that the man was being honored by his inclusion in something that was much larger and grander than himself. I doubt he felt honored during his years of blindness. But he has been greatly honored to have his story included in God's Word. These were new and humbling thoughts for me. This was the moment that I first became aware of the pride that was prevalent in my heart.

When something like the accident occurs in someone's life, it forces them to contemplate the possibility that they are not in control of their life. It is taboo in our modern-day world to even hint that someone is not in control of every facet of their life from the brand of cereal they buy to their gender. But regardless of what we think, the reality is that we are in control of very little. I have no more control over the aneurism in my carotid artery than whether the seeds that I plant in my garden will grow. I could be in peak physical condition, yet still develop ALS or discover the presence of a tumor. If you have kids, then you understand exactly what I mean. Regardless of what I say or threaten them with, if they want to disobey me, they will.

Looking back on my life, one word that comes to my mind is pride. I am a very prideful person. C.S. Lewis, in his book *Mere Christianity*, had this to say on the subject:

"According to Christian teachers, the essential vice, the utmost evil, is pride. Unchastity, anger, greed, drunkenness, and all that, are mere flea bites in comparison: it was through pride that the devil became the devil: pride leads to every other vice: it is the complete anti-God state of mind…

…it is pride which has been the chief cause of misery in every nation and every family since the world began."[9]

Even as I write that, I can feel counter arguments welling up within my mind. My "self" is preparing its rebuttal with numerous testimonies of times that I "did the right thing" or gave up my seat for someone in a waiting room. I could tell you how I personify each fruit of the spirit with relative ease.

Clearly, I did not have an accurate understanding of pride. I thought it was rather simple, bragging about oneself, making others feel inferior, putting others down, overconfidence, arrogance. But the truth is that pride is much more sinister and worse, camouflaged. The Lord has exposed a very real and deep running vein of pride in my heart. However, it was something that I was unable or unwilling to see for most of my life. You see, one of pride's greatest strengths is its invisibility. It comes cloaked in so many disguises that we fail to identify it for what it really is, a distorted love of self. My hope is that my experience, my journey, will help you to see the same vein of pride in your own heart. If you hear nothing else that I say hear this, the vein of pride runs through every soul. It began at the fall and will remain until we are made new by Christ.

The word I would use to describe my experience with this accident is "humbling."

The Lord knew exactly how to break the hold of pride in my heart. I have learned that there is a very effective tool at our disposal to expose and combat pride within our hearts; fasting. We tend to think of fasting as giving up food for a certain period of time, however, fasting can be giving up anything for even a short period of time. Fasting has been essential in identifying idols that I have erected in my heart and mind. When I was in rehab, I was furious when I was told that I could not listen to music. Music has long been a refuge for me, especially when I am angry. Due to my brain injuries my doctors were very careful to prevent overstimulation. Frankly, I did not care about that in the moment, I only thought about how listening to music would help me feel better and get some of my anger out. This fasting was not voluntary in any way, but it did help me to see that I had allowed music to become an idol.

The Spotted Lantern Fly

If you live in central PA, you know about the notorious Spotted Lantern Fly and chances are you really dislike them. They have become a nuisance in this area in recent years and everyone wants to destroy all of them. They are dangerous to our plant life and surrounding agricultural environment. Thankfully, our house hadn't seen any of these insects for a decent amount of the summer season, but then it happened; we encountered our first one on our back-screen door. We of course got rid of it, but it was very hard to kill something that could be seen as beautiful. The first time I saw the Spotted Lantern Fly the attractive red wings with black spots caught my eye as it flew by and reminded me of a majestic butterfly.

This is not unlike the things this world has to offer. This world offers bright, shiny, and beautiful things that are disguised, not showing their true dangerous nature. Things that can easily become an idol dressed in beautiful camouflage. We get sucked into these objects or activities but are unable or unwilling to kill them because of their exterior glamor. When we finally realize the danger that lurks underneath and are able to bring that to the surface, exposed to the light from above, can we choose to be free from the pests in our lives.

Anything I can't walk away from, or struggle to fast from, is at best being placed too much importance on and at worst has developed into an idol. Idolatry is someone or something that we love, desire, or want more than God. This could be literally anything, nothing is too small or insignificant. During my recovery I made it a point to fast from one thing each day. One day it was TV, the next it was coffee or unhealthy food, whatever I felt the Lord wanted me to give up that day. My prayer life was the strongest it had ever been as I was continually reminded that I needed to seek Christ's strength, rather than my own, to complete my daily fasting. I cannot emphasize how essential fasting was and has become for me.

A close friend told me after the accident that he believed I "would gain more than I lost." It absolutely did not feel like that at the time, but I can assure you that it is full of truth. While it is tempting to view an event like my accident as "bad," I think that would be a mistake. It is simply something that has happened to me and has the potential to produce positive and negative outcomes. Remember the blind man, how his life did not compare to the glory of God? If that does not humble us, then something is wrong. If God has been glorified through my accident, then how can I call it a bad thing? I will not do that. If God has been glorified then all that I and my family have gone through is worth it, I would not change the past if I could.

Your life, my life is of inestimable value, yet they do not compare to God's glory.

In every situation we can choose to trust that Christ is in control, seek Him in every storm.

Only by knowing who God is can we know who we are.

Accidents like this have a way of getting our attention. They confront us with how fragile life can be. They remind us that we can make plans, but those plans can change without any warning. The storms of life come without notice and they can be devastating. Just because we claim to be a believer and desire to walk with God, that does not exempt us from the trials of life. But there is one thing that was a great reminder to me as I went through one of the darkest times of my life. That reminder is that God's Word is a foundation. At the end of Jesus's Sermon on the Mount, in Matthew 7:24-27, Jesus sums up His teaching and brings His sermon to a close by saying that if you hear what I'm saying and apply it to your life, you are like a man who built a house on a rock. He compares this man with one who fails to hear and do. He says this man is like a man who built his house on sand. Both men are builders, but one builds on sure foundation, the other does not. Both experience the storms of life but only the man who

built on a sure foundation remains stand-
ing. To remain standing does not mean a
pain free life, a life without hardship. What
it means is that pain, trials, difficulties, and
suffering do not have to define us, though
they refine us. The storm can be great (big
enough to topple a house), but we can per-
severe through it when Jesus and His Word
are the foundation of our lives. Ben's acci-
dent is a powerful example of an unexpected
life storm. Seeing Ben hold on to Jesus is a
sure, solid, reliable, and dependable foun-
dation that holds us up in the storms of life.
I am extremely grateful that God brought
Ben through this terrible storm and is using
it to glorify Himself through Ben's life. And
no doubt, God has used this storm of life to
refine Ben and Lindsey (and many others
including myself) to let Him build our lives
upon Himself.

—Dan Krug (Ben's father)

Wrapped Up

Reflection Questions:

- Have you had any experiences with God that you cannot explain?

- Are there areas of your heart you have allowed bitterness and anger to permeate? Has holding onto these feelings given you power or control over the situation?

- Are there items in your life that you cannot give up? Are there signs that indicate these items could be idols? How is God calling you to remove these idols?

"But we have this treasure in jars of clay to show
that this all-surpassing power is from God and not
from us. We are hard pressed on every side, but not
crushed; perplexed, but not in despair; persecuted, but
not abandoned; struck down, but not destroyed."
2 Corinthians 4:7-9 (NIV)

Chapter 4

LIES IN THE DARKNESS

In the quiet, stillness of your heart, who's voice do you
hear? Do you hear the voices of those closest to you? Do
you hear the voices of the world? Your own voice? Satan's
voice? God's voice? Can we even tell those voices apart? For
the longest time I didn't comprehend the aspects and realness
of spiritual warfare. I knew that Satan was after me and my
family just because I accepted Christ as my Savior and now
had the Holy Spirit dwelling inside me. I didn't know that
evil would be lurking around in the darkness, picking apart
my every weakness, and whispering lies into my ear that sank
to my heart. I didn't understand why I believed such blatant
lies. I didn't understand the heavy spiritual weight placed
upon me. I didn't understand that I was under attack in the
most personal of ways. I didn't know how to hear God's voice

above all the others, including my own. I didn't know how to fight back.

I used to have this dream when I was younger that would come around every couple of months. I was in a large house with several rooms. The house was pitch black. A shadow would follow me into each room that I went into. The more it followed me the more scared I became. Then, as I entered one room a light came on and the shadow hid. The minute the light went off the shadow would attack again close enough I could feel its breath on the back of my neck. I fought against the shadow by turning on all the lights and lighting up the house until the shadow disappeared completely. I didn't fully understand the meaning behind this dream, if any, until I came upon this verse:

> "Be alert and of sober mind. *Your enemy the devil prowls around like a roaring lion looking for someone to devour.* Resist him, standing firm in the faith, because you know that the family of believers throughout the world is undergoing the same kind of suffering."
>
> 1 Peter 5:8-9 (NIV)

Satan loves to get individuals alone, isolated from the rest of the body. Isolated to stew over the many thoughts swirling in your mind. Isolated to believe that you are the only one who this is happening too, that you are the reason this is happening. Isolation and stillness can bring about thoughts that you never believed you could have, lies that twist and cut. "The thief comes only to steal and kill and destroy; I have come that they may have life and have it to the full" (John 10:10, NIV). The evil one loves to drain all the good out of our spirits and can even make us believe that life itself is so bad we can't walk in it anymore. To deplete all of our life, our prosperous and joyful life. Because when this happens, we are not whole, and cannot fulfill all that we are in Christ, all that He has for us to accomplish. "Satan cloaks his deceptions in a way that piques our feelings, excites our instincts, or brings to mind a past experience—all in a sly attempt at compelling us to move forward without consulting truth, veering us off course and outside of God's will."[10]

This is what I was about to walk into.

Without armor.

Without protection.

So, I believed…in the lie.

In just a few short months after the accident, in September 2015, I was to give birth to our first child. I didn't have any younger siblings, so babies were foreign to me. I never babysat infants when I was younger, and I can't say that as a little girl my dream was becoming a mom. But as I grew closer to Christ, and all that He calls me to be in this world, having a baby turned into a dream come true.

My pregnancy was one of ease, no morning sickness, no swelling, and only weight gain in my belly. This made me greedy and prideful. I of course, like most first-time moms, had a laundry list of unrealistic expectations that one hundred percent would come to fruition without a glitch… NOT! My mom never really shared with me what it was like to have a baby, so I was completely clueless. The disillusionment and disappointment from those expectations that I had built up in my head were too great for me to handle.

Labor and delivery was a total of twelve hours and our baby girl entered the world. She was amazing and beautiful, and I loved every aspect of those first few moments, but quickly those moments ended. I was so sick after the birth that I barely ate the entire time I was in the hospital. People came to see me and left and all the while I felt empty inside.

My brother-in-law told me years later that it was painful to visit me in the hospital after our daughter was born because I was physically there, but mentally distant, broken. I was a robot who moved and occasionally jumped into a conversation when prompted but was hollow inside, no soul to be found.

I envisioned how wonderful it would be to bring our baby home for the first time, just me, my husband, and our baby girl. After everything we had just been through it would be nice to have this precious moment together as a family. I didn't want anyone to stay and help with our daughter, after all, I was the mom and I could take care of my daughter, right? God did entrust her to me, right? I painted this picture in my head of how amazing that time with this new member of our family would be; I made that image an idol.

No one in my family nursed their babies and I wanted to be the first. I was stubbornly determined to provide this measure for my baby and pridefully wanted to be the first one in my family, to which the Lord humbled me in every aspect of that area. But, the lack of bond that I felt stemming from the frustration of nursing was crippling me from actually providing what my daughter needed, which was just my presence. She was healthy and strong, and it really didn't matter how she got her nourishment just as long as she got it. That was a hard pill to swallow in the moment.

The minute I got home I couldn't have been more wrong. I was lost, a total oblivious mess. We got home and placed our daughter, still in the car seat, on the floor and just stared at her, then at each other, and thought, *Now what?*

What's next? How do I make it through the next few seconds, few hours, few days?

I have always had one of those personalities that exaggerates the very essence of what is going on. When something happens in my life I quickly and easily believe that this moment in time, this very short moment in time, will last forever. I see that moment cast out over my life and living my life in this moment brings anxiety and fear. I project these moments as my forever future. It is hard for me to see that when hard times come, they will only last for a season and then a new season will take its place.

God promises this.

God shows us this in the seasons of the year. Each season that passes brings something new and fresh. It is not long before that season turns into the next season and the next set of trials, hardship, celebrations, etc. It had been a hard lesson for me to learn to take each second one at a time, to hold onto what is happening in the moment and to not be quick to picture my future life. We learned this when Ben had his accident, the realization that the future is not certain or guaranteed. If we start to project that the hard times that come our way will last forever, we will miss out on the joy in the second-by-second moments that God brings. We will miss out on the beautiful details of our life that God shows us. We will miss out on a life lived well. A life lived to the fullest. A life of pure joy.

Thankfully, due to the accident, Ben was not able to work and that meant that while I was on maternity leave for three months, he would be there with me and boy did I need that. For the first week I didn't sleep more than two to three hours, the entire week! And oh, did I learn that I love my sleep.

Nursing was NOT this "natural thing that just happens" like everyone was telling me. I spent more time with my pump than I did with my child as I was determined to give her the best nourishment possible and the world was feeding me the lie that if I didn't nurse my child then I was a horrible mother. So, I killed myself to make sure that I had enough milk so that my husband could feed our daughter while I pumped milk for the next feeding, pumping exclusively for three months.

You moms out there know how much sacrifice exclusively pumping requires and I commend all mothers for any method of feeding their babies. But, for me, this was slowly killing me from the inside out. It was a constant reminder that I was a failure because I couldn't do something as "natural" as feeding my baby. It was a lie that had been fed to me from the very beginning of my life. *You are NOT good enough.* You will never have a strong "bond" or relationship with your daughter. You will NOT be the generation breaker that God wants you to be. You will not, not, not.

I was not eating enough to keep going, sleeping enough to tame the exhaustion, and not strong enough to want to live. As evening approached my anxiety would heighten and I would start to feel my heart race and hear my mind swirl with the lies of the evil one. Satan had me right where he wanted me. Feeling alone, but not really. Feeling isolated, yet I had family members all around. Feeling like at any minute this very fine line that I was walking on would snap and I would crash to the ground.

This is one of the reasons that the Lord saved my husband, to be a presence in my time of need. He had been a believer his whole life and had a deeper connection with God. I was a newer believer who had just witnessed the most horrible tragedy in my life and was still trying to process all that had happened and grieve. Ben could only watch as he saw his wife slip into the deep and do nothing about it. The depression that I was facing was too strong for any human to bring me through. God and His Word was the only thing that could save me.

Before having a baby, I never experienced depression. I was usually pretty joyful and tried to love life. There were times that I got frustrated or sad but never a state of debilitating depression that left me wanting to never come out of my room again. Depression that made me not want to take care of my newborn baby. I didn't believe that there was any family history of depression that I had to worry about. I read about postpartum depression and some of the signs, but never believed that it could or would happen to me. I had a very smug attitude that because I had the Lord, He would save me from anything and even if I have postpartum, I wouldn't have to worry. It wouldn't be that bad.

As each evening approached after I had my daughter I worried. I never slept because my anxiety would keep me awake, keep my mind running in all different directions, keep my heart racing at an unbelievable pace. I could hear every thump in my chest beating at an alarmingly high audible. It was one of those things that is really hard to explain, how you think or the actions that you take. I remember being outside in the middle of the night just standing there telling my husband that the pain was too great, and I would give anything for the pain to stop. The scary part was, I didn't know how I got there. I was walking and talking like a normal person, but inside I was perishing.

Fear and anxiety crippled me, paralyzed me from fully being present for my little one. I was physically able to sustain her, but mentally I couldn't swim through years of dirt and debris to find the surface. I was drowning. I felt so alone in motherhood, as though no one else ever went through the struggles that I was going through. With the physical pain, the endless nights of not sleeping, and the mounting pressure of being this amazing mom I had envisioned, shame and guilt crept in at the realization of the disappointment that surrounded me. And as shame and guilt pulled me ever so slowly to the bottom, I was ready for the Lord to call me home, but by my own doing.

Growing up, without the presence of the Lord, the mere thought of death left me feeling anxious. I remember sitting in my room one night and thinking about the fact that one day I will not be here on this planet. I imagined a world were those around me were going about their business, but I was nowhere to be found. The unknown of what would happen to me after I was gone sent a shock through my entire body to the point where I was curled up having a panic attack. I didn't want to not be here with my parents, friends, those I loved. I didn't want to not be able to play sports, read books, partake in my hobbies and interests. I didn't know that there was a place that I could go to when I died that would be far greater than the best that I could possibly imagine here on earth.

When I became a believer, I learned that there doesn't have to be fear in dying because when we die, we will be with Jesus in Heaven and all pain, suffering, and turmoil would be gone forever. But selfishly, as my life after I first became a believer, wasn't filled with pain or suffering, I wasn't scared to die, but I didn't want to die. I didn't want to miss all the future opportunities that this world had to offer. The future career move that I may make. The future children I may have and being there to instill in them all that God would want me to. The future grandchildren that they may have that I may spoil and give all the love Christ would show. Now the fear was gone from the thought of death, but the timing needed to be much later in life, my timing.

But in this moment, this very scary moment, as exhaustion clouded my mind, anxiety ravaged my body, shame shattered my already damaged heart, and fear broke the only strand holding me together, I wanted to die! I wanted to leave this life and be with Jesus in Heaven. I wanted the pain to stop, the shame to be lifted, the guilt to be washed clean, and the fear to subside.

As a believer in Christ, I justified how easy leaving this world would be. After all, I knew where I was already going to end up. I had accepted Christ as my Savior and now I would be able to be with Him forever. The place that was always intended for me to live.

This was my momentary lapse of wanting to give in to evil temptations and I was oh so willing to give in. This was a lie that I wasn't good enough to be here, that the people around me didn't need me, so why stay? BUT this is NOT God's will! We have no idea what impact our lives, the stories that God writes on our hearts, can have in the future!

So, each night my husband would sit by my side and watch over me, ensuring that I didn't hurt myself in any way. And as he sat there, he read Psalms to me over and over until I would fall asleep and sleep eventually came. The reading of those Psalms declared that our house was a sanctuary for God, God only, and that Satan and his evil had no authority to be there. It was a proclamation of truth. These are some of the truths that resonated with me through these nights:

> *The Lord is my shepherd, I lack nothing.*
> *He makes me lie down in green pastures, He*
> *leads me beside quiet waters, He refreshes*
> *my soul. He guides me along the right paths*

*for His name's sake. Even though I walk
through the darkest valley, I will fear no
evil, for you are with me; your rod and your
staff, they comfort me. You prepare a table
before me in the presence of my enemies. You
anoint my head with oil; my cup overflows.
Surely your goodness and love will follow
me all the days of my life, and I will dwell
in the house of the Lord forever.*

Psalms 23 (NIV)

*The Lord is my light and my salva-
tion-whom shall I fear? The Lord is the
stronghold of my life-of whom shall I be
afraid? When the wicked advance against
me to devour me, it is my enemies and my
foes who will stumble and fall. Though an
army besiege me, my heart will not fear;
though war break out against me, even then
I will be confident.*

Psalms 27:1-3 (NIV)

*Keep me free from the trap that is set for
me, for you are my refuge. Be merciful to
me, Lord, for I am in distress; my eyes grow
weak with sorrow, my soul and body with
grief. My life is consumed by anguish, my
years by groaning; my strength fails because
of my affliction, and my bones grow weak.
My times are in your hands; deliver me
from the hands of my enemies, from those
who pursue me.*

Psalms 31:4, 9-10, 15 (NIV)

In those moments the Lord would wrap me in peace, calm my mind, slow my thoughts, and gently lay me down to sleep. Enough sleep that as each day passed, I would get stronger both physically and spiritually. God's Word would build into my mind and sink into my heart.

While there weren't physical enemies trying to end my physical life, evil was after my heart. Only God could save me from that evil, and He did, when I was willing to lay down my own pride, selfishness, and life. David sums up beautifully the first few days of my depression through his song of praise to the Lord, thanking God for delivering him from the hand of his enemies, including Saul. He captures the fear of the enemy swirling around me with the realness of spiritual warfare in my life and God coming to my rescue enveloping me in His peace and protection;

> *The Lord is my rock, my fortress and my deliverer; my God is my rock, in whom I take refuge, my shield and the horn of my salvation. He is my stronghold, my refuge and my savior-from violent people you save me. The waves of death swirled about me; the torrents of destruction overwhelmed me. The cords of the grave coiled around me; the snares of death confronted me. In my distress I called to the Lord; I called out to my God. From His temple He heard my voice; my cry came to His ears. He reached down from on high and took hold of me; He drew me out of the deep waters. He rescued me from my powerful enemy, from my foes, who were too strong for me. You save the humble, but your eyes are on the haughty to*

bring them low. You, Lord are my lamp; the Lord turns my darkness into light.

2 Samuel 22:2-3, 5-7,
17-18, 28-29 (NIV)

For weeks, that turned into months, I would slip back into this world of darkness. I would have good days and then Satan would remind me of something that brought me right back to feeling like a failure as a mom and woman and then the sleepless nights would return. In some ways the anxiety felt like the thorn in my side that just wouldn't go away, popping up at just the right moment in my life when I fixed my eyes on the Lord and things started to turn around. "Therefore, in order to keep me from becoming conceited, I was given a thorn in my flesh, a messenger of Satan, to torment me. Three times I pleaded with the Lord to take it away from me. But He said to me, 'My grace is sufficient for you, for my power is made perfect in weakness'" (2 Corinthians 12:7-9a, NIV).

I was suffering and didn't understand why the Lord wasn't answering the questions that I was raising to Him. Paul Tripp, in his book *Suffering,* makes this comparison with Job and the suffering that he went through:

"When Job, who had lost everything, asked God for a reason for his suffering, seeking answers that we all tend to cry out for in the devastation of hardship, God didn't give answers (See Job 38-41). Rather than giving Job answers he wouldn't understand and that his heart couldn't contain, God answered Job by pointing to himself, to his presence, power, and glory. *He knew that Job's instinct was to seek answers, when what Job really needed was to seek God.*"[11]

God showed me that as important as giving me a thorn in my side I can't forget that there is a second part to that 2

Corinthians verse. "Therefore, I will boast all the more gladly about my weaknesses, so that Christ's power may rest on me. That is why, for Christ's sake, I delight in weaknesses, in insults, in hardships, in persecutions, in difficulties. *For when I am weak, then I am strong*" (2 Corinthians 12:9b-10, NIV). The answer is to seek God. To daily lay down all of our difficulties and seek the Lord as our refuge and strength. Because when the world sees weakness in our suffering, the Lord sees strength, wisdom, compassion, understanding, love, and joy.

I would end up going to see a Christian counselor to seek out what was really going on and hear me when I say that there is NO shame in getting professional help. Seeking out counseling was one of the most freeing experiences in my life. No one around me could understand the things that my counselor could point me to.

I knew that this wasn't just about not being able to nurse my child or the bond that would inevitably be stronger than I could ever imagine through our years together. This would be about my heart and the underlying issues from my past, the deeper-rooted issues that I had suppressed for many years.

I was helped by my counselor to realize, when I had a baby girl of my own, my first child ever, that my greatest fear was repeating the same relational mistakes I had seen over the decades. I was so determined to be a generation breaker, which fueled most of my parenting fears in the first few months. Everything that had happened, all the disappointments that I was facing, all stemmed from this deeper-rooted issue. I didn't want my daughter to have a broken relationship with me. I didn't want my love to be conditional with her. I wanted her to grow up to be my best friend, for her to know that she would always be my first priority, that she was worthy just because of who God made her to be. I wanted that unbreakable bond and I realized that I needed to grieve the fact that I didn't have this in my past. I was trying so hard to make it right with my daughter, over trying really, that my anxiety and depression stole the very thing that I longed to achieve, and my life.

My counselor helped me to see that just having Jesus as my Savior already changes the dynamics of our relationship. That I was trying too hard to control all the things that I needed to give to God, that He was already in control of. I was helped to see that I can't possibly give my daughter grace if I can't learn to give myself the grace that God freely gives me. That I didn't have to earn that grace. That my relationship with my daughter was already made different purely from the fact that I have the Holy Spirit, helping me to make decisions based on following a God-centered path. She asked me what it would be like for me to just be me, not striving for perfection or working so hard to please everyone around me; to which I answered that I wouldn't even know what that looked like.

I remember one of the first times I went to church after having our little one. As the worship songs started to play the heaviness of shame flooded my body and tears poured down my face. The weight of the gazing eyes around me filled me with guilt. I couldn't let them see I was struggling at this new mom thing. I had compared myself to all of my friends who seemingly had no issues adjusting to motherhood.

My pride trapped me from being vulnerable and real to those closest to me and opportunities that God presented to help put the pieces back together passed me by. I was marooned on an island of low self-esteem and pride. But God sent a rescue ship to my island. One by one members of our church family, women and mothers who I had admired and respected for years, stepped onto my island to share their stories. Their stories of hardship and redemption. Their stories of realness and hope. Their stories of how Jesus rescues.

Around this same time, I started attending the ladies Bible study at my church. I had never attended this group before but as life for me was changing an opportunity to be a part of this ministry opened up and opened up for a specific reason. God in His infinite wisdom opened a door to a Bible study that I desperately needed to hear. The study was *Armor of God* by Priscilla Shirer.

> *Finally, be strong in the Lord and in His mighty power. Put on the full armor of God, so that you can take your stand against the devil's schemes. For our struggle is not against flesh and blood, but against the rulers, against the authorities, against the powers of this dark world and against the spiritual forces of evil in the heavenly realms. Therefore put on the full armor of God, so that when the day of evil comes, you may be able to stand your ground, and after you have done everything, to stand. Stand firm then, with the belt of truth buckled around your waist, with the breastplate of righteousness in place, and with your feet fitted with the readiness that comes from the gospel of peace. In addition to all this, take up the shield of faith, with which you can extinguish all the flaming arrows of the evil one. Take the helmet of salvation and the sword of the Spirit, which is the word of God.*
>
> Ephesians 6:10-17 (NIV)

This study gave me the tools that God designed to be used against the enemy. It gave me an understanding of the magnitude of spiritual warfare. The study helped to show me that I needed to put on my full armor that God had already equipped me with to fight back against the evil one that was trying to bring me down and destroy me. "Satan knows that if you'll ever push past the insecurity or doubt or fear that's burning in your soul, choosing instead to believe the truth of God and walk in accordance with it, you'll erect a shield of protection that will smother his plans."[12]

The study taught me that I needed to put on my shoes of peace.

"Shalom, does not refer to the absence of chaos, but rather to an overall, deeply entrenched sense of harmony, health, and wholeness in the midst of chaos. In fact, true peace is best detected and measured against the backdrop of commotion and confusion—when instability abounds, yet you remain steadfast; when disappointment and confusion are near, yet you're still capable of walking with Spirit-infused confidence, stability, and steadiness. That's how you know your feet are fitted "with the preparation of the gospel of peace"—a peace beyond comprehension."[13]

At this point I'm thinking, *Okay, Satan I am ready for you to go pick on someone else. You can leave me and my family alone and let us relax for a bit with the whole "devastating events of our lives" thing.* What I realized was that by growing closer to God, I am making the enemy angry and he will try everything he can to not lose me to God. I learned that if I am truly investing my heart and soul and giving it over to God, I will be persecuted and sought after by evil. But if I am willing, I can use these moments of persecution to bring others alongside, showing them how to put on the full armor of God, and teaching them how to stand and fight.

But you know, the thing that resonated with me the most was that through all the persecution and devastation, by building a strong bond with Christ alone, honoring Him with all that I am, and being transparent with myself, those around me, and God, I have never felt freer in my entire life! Free from the weight of the shame! Free from the regret of the guilt! Free from the clutches of anxiety and depression! Free and unparalyzed to fully live life!

> "Do not be afraid of what you are about
> to suffer. I tell you, the devil will put
> some of you in prison to test you, and
> you will suffer persecution for ten days.
> Be faithful, even to the point of death,
> and I will give you a life as your victor's
> crown."
>   Revelation 2:10 (NIV)

Wrapped Up

Reflection Questions:

- Have there been experiences or expectations in your life that have left you disillusioned and disappointed? How have you dealt with that and where have you turned for healing?

- In what areas do you feel alone, isolated from others? Do you believe that no one else is going through what you struggle with? Do you feel shame?

- When in isolation, do you spend more time and energy trying to keep your situation hidden or pursuing transparency and fellowship? Why?

- "If I didn't nurse my child then I was a terrible mother." What do you allow to define you? Is this identity coming from God or man?

- In what ways has fear robbed you of joy?

"Always be joyful. Never stop praying. Give thanks
no matter what happens. God wants you to thank
Him because you believe in Christ Jesus. Don't try
to stop what the Holy Spirit is doing. Don't treat
prophecies as if they weren't important. But test all
prophecies. Hold on to what is good. Say no to every
kind of evil. God is the God who gives peace."
1 Thessalonians 5:16-23a (NIRV)

Chapter 5

NEVER STOP PRAYING

His face was ghostly white. Through his eyes you could
see to his soul, hollow, empty. I had never seen this
man so defeated. This strong pillar of our family, one whom
I had only seen cry once in my thirty years. One who never
showed his true emotions was now crying out from deep
within. The burden he was facing was too much for him to
handle and he was about to walk into the building that stood
before him for help. A building that he would never have
found himself standing outside of. My heart ached for him.
Ben and I had prayed for twelve years for this moment. I
knew what he needed, but he would have to walk through
the lesson in order to reach it. I knew it would be hard, painful, scary. He would walk a path and go through a storm that

I had just come out of. I knew he was scared, fearful about the outcome of the next twenty-four hours, if he would even make it through. I knew what it would take, but could only watch, wait, support, and pray.

Growing up, my dad was always my guy. He was a strong and tough man, little emotion if any, but very supportive. He was and is one of the most hardworking men that I have ever known. Constantly keeping himself busy with his job, yard or housework, and sports on the weekend; I practically grew up on a softball field. My dad isn't one to take a break. Not from work, not from life. So, when he was forced to slow down after some shoulder surgery, be still, and rest in life he fell to pieces, down the same trap that I had fallen into, believing the same lies that I believed.

Up until this point, from the view of the daughter, my family's life had been one of predictability. We went about each day, living for the day, living for the world, living for ourselves. I was always taught to work really hard, get a good paying job, save money to buy whatever you may want, and coast out life until retirement. Don't get me wrong, there is absolutely nothing wrong with a strong work ethic, in fact God calls us to be laborers in Genesis 2:15 (NIV), "The Lord God took the man and put him in the Garden of Eden to work it and take care of it." But the question is, who are we working hard for? Are we hard workers to honor and glorify God in all that we say and do because He asks us to? Or are we hard workers, striving for the next big achievement to glorify man, this world, ourselves? Colossians 3:23-24 (NIV) says, "Whatever you do, work at it with all your heart, as working for the Lord, not for human masters, since you know that you will receive an inheritance from the Lord as a reward. It is the Lord Christ you are serving."

As a child, God was not part of our family equation. On Sundays, instead of church, we would play softball at a tournament somewhere on the East Coast. In most ways we lived very consumeristic lives. Sure, money was tight when I was younger, but as I got older if we needed something or wanted something my parents did what they could to provide it. They sacrificed a lot to make sure that I had new softball equipment and went to the best showcases to further pursue my collegiate softball career. My parents both had quality jobs, very stable, that paid a decent amount of money. They had truly worked hard to get to this point in their lives.

Retirement was around the corner for them if they just kept to the plan that my dad had devised. Nothing wrong with any of this, per say, but when we believe that we alone are accomplishing this and devise our own hard and fast plans, therein lies the trouble. I could work as hard as anyone else to be a concert pianist (my dream career) but if God hasn't provided that skill, if that's not what He has in my future, then it will never come to be. God's plans do not always, if ever, equal my plans!

This life we lived, full of consistency, luxuries, and expectancies was just where the evil one wanted us. Because if we were here in this place, not having difficulties, why on earth would we need to turn to a Savior? Absolutely NO reason at all! This is one of the most dangerous places to be as human beings. The complacency zone. The place where all is good and agreeable in your life and help is not needed from anyone on the outside, a very prideful way of thinking and a hard lesson to learn how to let someone help. Where our thoughts are, *Well, I have worked hard enough up until this point to get exactly where I wanted, things are comfortable so I will make it work the rest of the way. I will set a plan until the end.* And when that plan that we so precisely worked out, and worked so hard to achieve, comes crashing down, when all our hopes and dreams shatter and we are filled with disappointments, we don't know how to process all the emotions that surge through us and we crack.

As a Lebanon County, mostly known as "stubborn dutchmen," born and raised family, we do NOT like change. We don't know how to navigate the unknown. It's scary and lonely at times. It shatters all realms of our small, sheltered lives. This is how I felt when change hit my life. This is what I saw when change hit my dad's life; when God shook up our picture perfect "Etch A Sketched" lives.

My dad was fifty-three years old and years of playing slow-pitch softball had deteriorated his shoulder leaving pain and numbness throughout his arm. He had put off having surgery, in typical dad fashion, until it was absolutely necessary. Which came during a very cold winter. He would need to take months off work for recovery and rehabilitation as his job required the ability to physically lift fifty pounds up over his head. This meant that he couldn't be lifting and doing chores or work around the house. This meant that he would need to be still, calm, rest his body and rest his mind. This meant that his mind would have time to think and spiral.

When our minds have time to think, when the weight of the world swirling around inside our brains is lifted, it can be a very enlightening and peaceful time or it can be a time where all you have stuffed deep within comes surging to the forefront and is too overwhelming to handle. This is where we had landed, outside this building, the one that would help my dad process and navigate the decades of emotional turmoil he had come to realize he built up deep inside.

Up until this time, and after I had given my life to Christ, Ben and I would talk about God or what having a relationship with Christ looked like with my parents, but we would almost always get a door slammed in our face and a wall built back up. Ben and I would try to knock one brick of that wall down only to have five more bricks go back up, so we would tread lightly around the subject of God.

Then, the accident happened and our faith, and those that were closest to us, came bursting forth. There was no way to hide our relationships with Christ and all the worship, prayer, and power that went along with that relationship, especially in the most devastating of times. My parents saw something through us and around us that they had never seen before, TRUST and PEACE in the only One that could get us through. That was one of the first times my mom told me that she was proud of me and didn't know how I was handling things with such peace and grace.

Three years after the accident, our church had asked Ben and I to give our testimonies at the Easter service. The service was themed around God's grace. We were to share God's grace in the events that happened in our lives as there were quite a few at that point and more coming literally during the exact moments we were sharing God's story. Our church had three Easter services that year and I had invited my parents to come to at least one of those services to hear how God had worked in and through our lives. They had only occasionally come to a service at our church for the holidays but at the time wouldn't give a second thought to coming every week.

It's hard to describe how I was feeling when I asked them. I wanted so badly for my parents to come hear these "God moments" and be proud of me for just getting up there and being vulnerable in front of nearly two thousand people. My heart ached for their approval. At the age of twenty-eight I was still looking for anything outside of sports to make them proud.

As each service went by, and my parents still not there, my heart broke into more and more pieces. Probably the most exhilarating moment of my life up until this point where I was going well outside my comfort zone to give all glory to God and to show how good He is in the midst of tragedy, and they missed all three services. I was angry with them. Which made it even more difficult when my dad called me in between two services leaving me a desperate voicemail, a plea for help.

A couple months before my dad had his shoulder surgery he was in good spirits about the whole situation. Little did he know that attitude and feeling would quickly change. I had gone with my mom to the hospital taking my young daughter to sit and wait until my dad went back to surgery, not easy with a little one, but I knew that my mom needed that support and I knew it would be an opportunity to pray with them both. A few weeks after, I would take my dad to a couple of his therapy appointments, we got my dad set up with an exercise machine to keep him occupied while he was home by himself, and my daughter and I would visit frequently to help the days go a little quicker. After all, I was used to that as I had just become a stay-at-home mom for the first time and the days in the winter were long!

Things were going well for my dad with therapy and him being home from work, despite not being able to work around the house, but like all man-made plans, they tend to fall through, and God's plan comes to light in ways we never expect or frankly want.

My dad started to have some physical setbacks and those physical setbacks started to take a toll on him mentally and emotionally. He became unable to sleep, and with exhaustion came anxiety, and with anxiety came depression. The same state and cycle that the Lord had allowed me to go through just two years prior to this moment so I knew exactly how my dad felt. Day after day my dad would tell me that he didn't sleep the night before and each time he didn't sleep the anxiety would build.

When it was time for my dad to finally go back to work, he was physically ready, but not emotionally or mentally ready. He still wasn't sleeping and had to get up early in the morning to go to work. Since we don't like change in our family and our culture, when one doesn't get the "normal" amount of sleep, the number that they always get each and every night, panic ensues. My dad would lay there watching the clock fearing the inevitable tick tock of the arms until the morning, which brought exhaustion. Then, he had to go to work on top of this and perform manual maintenance, hard work with no room for grogginess. So, in order to get that adequate amount of sleep, in numbers, he required a sleeping pill for aide, which in our family is a big issue. We were never ones to take any sort of medication mainly out of fear of what it would do to our bodies and the side effects. We stuck it out and suffered through the pain until our bodies naturally fought off the sickness. That was the proud Hoerner way of doing it, all by ourselves.

Following the same path that I had just come out of showed me that getting an "adequate" amount of sleep didn't come in numbers. If I was truly trusting in the Lord to give me the strength, He could and would give me that with even just two hours. That my perception of what "normal" was may not be "normal" for me. And that is okay! I might be tired, oh yes, tired to the point where I couldn't make it another second. But God got me through. He got me through on eight hours of sleep, if that would ever happen again after kids, and He got me through multiple nights of only two hours of sleep.

How much of a coincidence is it then that my dad was running the same marathon that I had just finished? Absolutely none! This was God allowing me to go through some of the hardest times in my life to bring this man, this father, the man that had always taught me, to the ultimate teacher Himself. And the Lord, as always, had greater plans than I or my dad could imagine.

Over the years from the accident to this moment in my dad's life, I could slowly start to see my dad's heart soften. It was subtle at first. Showing more affection for my kids than I had seen before, giving up more of his time, just stopping by to say hello and see the kiddos, the way he talked to me, the look on his face when my kids would run up to him shouting grandpa, his general being. You could see God moving in his heart, he just needed one last push to fully let go of control and give his life over to Christ.

The sleeping pills worked for a short time but brought other complications to my dad's physical health. As the abnormal sleep patterns continued, the anxiety built, and as the anxiety built it brought a spell of depression that knocked my dad off his feet. Ben and I would go see my dad every day to help shepherd him back into the light from his dark pit of despair. I was fearful that he would do something drastic to make the pain stop permanently. I knew what he was feeling, I had felt that same feeling almost two years earlier. The depression got to such a low point that my dad had checked himself into a mental health facility for a day program, the building my dad found himself standing in front of almost paralyzed to walk through the front door. The building that I would never have thought I would ever be visiting my parent in. The building that could yield so much good but hold so much shame at the same time.

Ben and I knew what my dad needed; he needed a Savior. Not a medical savior, the One and only Savior. Each day we would see my dad he would tell us the same story. The same ailments, the same fears, the same worries, the same problems, the same lies. And each day, instead of shoving God in his face, which we knew was the answer, we held back. We prayed with him, but we didn't immerse my dad in the hope of Jesus Christ.

After about a week, Ben and I were both mentally exhausted from taking care of our little one and also taking care of my dad's mental and emotional health and trying to help my mom navigate this new scenario. I was tired of hearing the same thing over and over knowing that if my dad just gave up his life and put it in God's hands the Holy Spirit would start to change my dad from the inside. His circumstances might not be over instantly but his heart, his perspective, his outlook would start to be shaped and molded by the Holy Spirit.

Think about what I just wrote. I was tired of hearing the same thing over and over knowing that if my dad just gave up his life and put it in God's hands the Holy Spirit would start to change him from the inside. How easy that is to say when you are looking at someone else's life, but oh how hard it is to carry out in your own life. We do this all the time! I do this all the time! Take my woes to God over and over, the same things, never FULLY giving my life to the Lord, never completely trusting that God is good and so are His plans. But oh, what would life look like if we truly did this with all our hearts!

Ben and I had felt that the Lord was calling us to lay aside all of our reservations, all of our filters, and share with my dad whatever the Lord gave us to say. I was no longer concerned that my words would hurt my dad's feelings or would be used to build his wall back up that was slowly starting to crumble. I was going to share everything that God led me to share to pierce the heart of that brick wall in one punch. And for the first time in my thirty years I had a real, authentic, deeply personal conversation with my earthly father. And to my surprise, in his moment of desperation, that conversation was a two-way street, received with the utmost respect for me, for what I believed, and for God!

After the second Easter service was finished, I finally listened to the voicemail from my dad. He sounded lost and confused, as if all hope was gone. He needed my help, help from one of our pastors! After twelve years of prayer, a missed opportunity to hear what God had done in our lives, and countless occasions where the gospel of Jesus was shared, my dad was asking to seek counsel from one of our pastors! I had mixed emotions of sadness for how painful things had gotten for my dad and joy that this moment had finally come. Of course, if he had been at the Easter service, he could have just walked up to a pastor and talked to them, but life isn't that simple. Ben and I tried to get in touch with any church staff member that would pick up their phone as we knew there was a short window of opportunity to capitalize on this pivotal moment. When we finally got to talk to our senior pastor and explain what was going on with my dad and that he desperately needed to talk to him, our pastor didn't miss the opportunity to lead his flock. He finished up his time with his family and met with both of my parents a few hours later. And Ben and I let go of my dad and left him in the capable hands of God.

Trust and respect are hard things to come by, especially if you have a tainted view of a trustworthy symbol. And my parents definitely had a tainted view of all things church and church leaders. But our pastor shattered all perceptions of those twisted views and showed my parents the true love of Christ. He would continue meeting with my parents on a weekly basis. I never knew what they would talk about, but God was putting each piece of the puzzle together, in His time. Our pastor had encouraged my parents to be open to exposing their deepest wounds and share secrets that were kept for over thirty years!

It's amazing how your perceptions on situations in your life, attitudes that you have, bitterness that you have harnessed can all change instantly when you know the end of the story. This is what happened to me. For decades, I had felt unfavored by my mother, put behind my older brother. Even after watching him make wrong choice after wrong choice I felt that my mother always gravitated toward him.

I had always envied that.

I had never felt good enough.

I harnessed bitterness toward my mother and my brother, but then I learned a new piece of information.

A piece of information that had been kept for decades that opened my eyes to why I had felt second best all my life. My brother was really my half-brother. My brother was the one thing that held my mom together all those years ago in her darkest moments. My brother was her life, was the reason she could take one breath after another. He gave her purpose to live.

While I don't know the whole story, nor is it mine to tell, this information helped me to grieve the feelings and relationship that my mom and I had all our lives. My mom showed courage for having and raising a child as a single parent and giving my brother life as God intended. My dad showed grace in adopting my brother not caring about the hurt of the past or the unknown of the future.

This information helped me forgive and move forward, to lay down my bitterness. But what I learned was that we cannot rely on knowing the whole story to be able to forgive and move forward because we will never fully know the ending. All those years of a broken relationship and bitterness made the enemy ecstatic. He loved the fact that I wasted so much of my time being angry, not able to give grace, not able to forgive because that state pulled me away from God. It is a choice to forgive, and no not an easy choice. Even after learning the truth, the whole story, it was hard to forgive, but necessary to grow my relationship with not only my mom, but with Christ as well.

From that moment on my parents started to come to church, every Sunday, and slowly started to get involved in the extracurricular activities that our church had to offer. A few short months later, I received another phone call from my dad, but this one would be a life changer. He called to tell me that he had given his life to the Lord and accepted Jesus as his personal Savior! I was speechless. I never thought that this day would come and here it was before us. I think that I may have been more excited than my dad. For years I had wanted to be a witness to someone, to be a part of their story, their journey to Christ. I had heard of so many people who helped others come to the Lord and what that experience was like, but I never experienced that moment for myself, until now. And what a person to experience it with.

As children we are to be the ones to follow our parents, obey their commands, learn from them and their mistakes, be guided by them to the Lord. As the daughter I never thought that I would be the one to play the role as the teacher and guider to not only my children but my parents as well. Oh, but what a proud moment that was as a daughter of the heavenly Father to walk with my earthly father guiding him to our Lord and Savior! To God be all the glory for that one!

While we may give up, God will never! It was disheartening after praying for so long to no avail. Waiting in the unknown took a toll on my faith. I often questioned if God could or would really answer the "impossible" prayer, if He were big enough for that. At times, when things looked like they were going backwards more often than forwards hope started to be lost. And when my human disbelief was at an all-time high, God was merely asking, "Do you really trust me Lindsey? And my timing?"

If my dad would have gone through all of this any earlier in our lives, I would not have been able to help him. I wouldn't have been ready! I wasn't strong enough in my faith to build into someone else. I *was* still learning and growing myself; I *am* still learning and growing. I wanted to witness to others and bring them to the Lord, but the truth is, I needed to be brought to the Lord with my whole heart. I needed to hit rock bottom in my faith to be able to turn and rely solely on God not only in the times of suffering but in every situation, in everyday living. I needed to be humbled. God was softening my dad's heart through this journey and shaping mine.

Nothing is too hard for God. Nothing is outside of His reach. No prayer is too large, no request too grand. When you feel like you have prayed enough and the time has come to move on, pray harder and bolder. Do not be afraid to take all you are and all you have to God. He's not surprised by what you say or ask. He already knows your heart. "You have searched me, Lord, and you know me. You know when I sit and when I rise; you perceive my thoughts from afar. You discern my going out and my lying down; you are familiar with all my ways. Before a word is on my tongue you, Lord, know it completely. You hem me in behind and before, and you lay your hand upon me" (Psalms 139:1-5, NIV).

For about fifteen years I watched, waited, and prayed as my parents went about their lives. When all hope was seemingly lost, I witnessed God perform yet another miracle, as He softened the hearts of my parents and changed them in unimaginable ways. They were no longer lost children looking for their Father; they had been found and they came running like the prodigal son. I saw God's love in their spirit. I experienced God's love flowing forward out of their hearts. After fifty-five years of life, my parents were made new in Christ!

Wrapped Up

*For additional resources on forgiveness read 2 Corinthians 2:5-11 and prayer read Daniel 10.

Reflection Questions:

- Is there someone in your life that God is calling you to never stop praying for?

- When you do not see immediate results from your prayers how do you respond? Do you feel unheard? Read Daniel 10:12-14, how does this chapter challenge your posture towards God's "silence" in unanswered prayer?

- Can the Lord use the suffering in your life to bless someone else? If yes, does that challenge your attitude towards your suffering?

- Is there undealt with bitterness in your heart? What would it look like for you to present this to Jesus and ask Him to help you grieve and be free from it?

- Could the busyness of your life be a subconscious attempt to distract yourself from uncomfortable areas of your life?

"'For I know the plans I have for you,' declares the Lord, 'plans to prosper you and not to harm you, plans to give you hope and a future. Then you will call on me and come and pray to me, and I will listen to you. You will seek me and find me when you seek me with all your heart.'"

Jeremiah 29:11-13 (NIV)

Chapter 6

AN UNEXPECTED CALLING

I was sitting in the middle of the living room floor. My two kids, both under five, were playing all around me, but I couldn't hear them. I just sat there, physically present but emotionally stuck in my own little make-believe world. Emotionally, not even able to stand and help my son get his ball. Emotionally, not even able to play "family" with my daughter. Emotionally drained and angry.

I had wanted this life so badly. The words, more like lies, "be careful what you wish for" ringing in my ears. I had wanted to prove to those around me that this was where God was calling me to be even if they didn't understand my decisions and that I was worthy of this task that was so unnatural for me. I had wanted to prove to myself that I could have confidence in this area of my life and that I could handle this new lifestyle.

So why in the midst of all I ever thought that I wanted, all that God would want me to do, all that I had prayed for in the past two years did I feel so forlorn, so overwhelmed, so worthless?

I believe this happens a lot to first time moms. The desire to stay home with their children, only to finally get to that point and realize that it's not at all what they expected it to be. The job requires constant sacrifice, total selflessness. A job outside of our human nature. God doesn't just call us to keep our children alive. He calls us to make disciples out of them, to guide their hearts away from their selfish nature and toward a loving and selfless God. This was anything but what I had in mind when I signed up to leave my very lucrative job and stay home full time.

As a result of the accident, and the time away from work Ben needed to heal, paired with his company being sold at the exact same time, he lost his job. Not that it mattered in the moment as he wasn't able to work, and we didn't know if he would ever work again. I was thankfully at an amazing job that not only allowed me time away, with pay, to take care of Ben but also allowed me to still take my maternity leave for three months at the end of that same year, and my wonderful boss lobbied for individuals at our facility to donate extra vacation days so that I would be covered in the event that I needed more paid time; praise God the donations were maxed out!

So, I had a baby and went on maternity leave for three months and while on that leave I received a call from my new boss that he wanted me to apply for a promotional position. I couldn't believe that even while I was away, they were still thinking of me for a position that was next in line for my climb to the top. But as my leave was coming to an end, I didn't even want to go back at all, let alone to a new position in which I would have to learn everything about the entire operation at our facility. Because of my nature and personality, and the way I was raised to be a go-getter, and because goals in your job were what we lived for, I immediately, but reluctantly agreed.

If you would have asked me even six years ago, right before I had my first child, if I would have ever thought I would be a stay-at-home mom I would have said no in a heartbeat. That was not in my nature, to be a patient nurturer, but I love how Lysa Terkeurst talks about choosing to live that way by positioning her heart toward Christ; "I may not be gentle by nature, but I can be gentle by obedience."[14] I am not a nurturer by nature, but I can be nurturing by obedience (I encourage you to insert your own attribute and remember that by obedience in God that statement can become true)!

I didn't see that natural nurturing from the women in my family and I honestly was a very selfish, impatient person. I wanted what I wanted, and I worked hard to get it was my mindset. But I knew that was not what God wanted. I knew that He needed me to be there for my children and I wanted to be the one to raise them. So, my husband and I decided that if we could make ends meet financially, one of us would stay home with the kids full time and since I was the "breadwinner" in the family I knew before we even had kids that my husband would be the one to be a stay-at-home dad and I would continue going to work. At the time, that was okay with me. I didn't give it a second thought until those built up emotions from my past came flooding back after I had my daughter.

So, since Ben wasn't able to work and my three-month leave was up and a new job was awaiting me, I went back to work. And every day I went in I felt farther and farther away from my child. I was with my daughter every second that I could be, but with a higher status comes a higher amount of responsibilities. I worked in a factory and that was a twenty-four seven, three hundred and sixty-three day out of the year job (we were usually only closed on Thanksgiving and Christmas). I was in charge of the food safety for the entire plant so there was no slacking on the job, not that I would anyway.

I killed myself for that job. I rarely ever took breaks and worked extremely long hours. I was left feeling disheartened. Disheartened that I wasn't there for my child, even though I was there every second outside of work. Disheartened because I felt as though I missed the entirety of my daughter's life in those first years, that I was the worst mom ever because I rarely did anything alone with my daughter. And if I'm being honest, I was petrified to be alone with my daughter. I constantly felt unqualified and scared that something traumatic would happen to her and it would be my ineptness to blame. Disheartened every time my work phone rang and someone at my job needed more from me.

All of these feelings added to the stress of my already stressful life and eventually my heart broke. I wasn't sleeping, I cried literally every day. It was a complete nightmare. I didn't know or even understand how to balance my time between work and kids and what was worse was that I never made time to be still with God.

Reading the Bible went out the window. I was so exhausted that I always fell asleep when I tried to pray. I wasn't involved with my church and rarely made time to focus on myself. I was too busy fearing man and trying to please those around me. This was not only crushing my relationship with my daughter; it was tearing apart my relationship with Christ.

Are we using or abusing the time that God is providing for us?

We all say it. "I don't have enough time to get into God's Word." "There are too many things that I have to do and no way that I can sit and be still or quiet with the Lord." "Well, five minutes isn't enough time to get anything out of reading the Bible, so I just won't even bother if I know I won't get more time." "I am too exhausted to even think about praying so I will just hop on social media instead."

I know I have said these many times. Life is busy, yes, but life here on earth is not the priority, important yes, but not the goal. When I was working a full-time job and then coming home to take care of and spend time with my child, I never had enough time to be with God, so I would make the excuse. We make the excuse that there isn't enough time to give to God, but what are we doing with the time that God does give us? Because He gives us plenty of time and opportunities to be still with Him and read His Word. Are we using that time to further God's kingdom or are we abusing that time to place some other idol there instead? I was definitely an abuser of that time. I would waste the time that God would give and justify the reasoning behind why it was okay. A few minutes of "relaxation" would turn into an hour or so and before I knew it that precious time that God gave me would be gone, replaced with some insignificant idol. We need to be straight and honest with ourselves and ask what the most important thing in our lives is. We can see what that is by what we are doing with all the time God has given us.

I was bitter.
I was miserable with everything and everyone.
I was left with the overwhelming feeling of worthlessness.

I was angry with God that the one thing I thought was good and that He would want me to fulfill wasn't a possibility at this moment. At *this* moment. I would have to wait. Wait for God's perfect timing.

Waiting is one of the most difficult things to do, especially when you are waiting for something you believe that God would want you to do or have. The waiting can be cataclysmal. The waiting has the power to make you throw away years of faith and trust in God. The waiting has the power to make you throw caution to the wind, take life into your own hands, and make some drastic decisions to best fit your plans. When has that ever worked out in our favor? But that's where I was, waiting.

In Acts 1, after Jesus had just appeared to many people for forty days, He ascended to Heaven but promised to send them the Holy Spirit. "On one occasion, while He was eating with them, He gave them this command: 'Do not leave Jerusalem, but wait for the gift my Father promised, which you have heard me speak about. For John baptized with water, but in a few days you will be baptized with the Holy Spirit'" (Acts 1:4-5, NIV).

Now, Jesus doesn't tell them in a specific number of days the Holy Spirit will come, He just says a few days. The disciples would have to wait and trust that the Lord, after witnessing all that He had just accomplished, would send the Holy Spirit. Imagine their reactions! Jesus, who has just been resurrected and walking around witnessing to people leaves you and promises to send a gift of the Holy Spirit, but the catch is you have to wait! In Acts 1:7-8 (NIV), Jesus says to the disciples, "It is not for you to know the times or dates the Father has set by His own authority. But you will receive power when the Holy Spirit comes on you; and you will be my witnesses in Jerusalem, and in all Judea and Samaria, and to the ends of the earth." Do you think the disciples ever doubted that the Holy Spirit would come? Imagine if the disciples got tired of waiting, gave up, and left Jerusalem! They would have totally missed out on the final piece of the Trinity puzzle that every human being in the future would need to possess to stay connected to God. Imagine if we tried to move forward in this world without the Holy Spirit!

As the days turned into weeks, which turned into over a year, I waited for God to show me what was next. I hated going to work each day, but I was still going and giving all I had because that is what the Lord wants us to do. To do things not just for the sake of doing them but to be grateful and do them for the Lord. I thought that I was making time for God and giving Him "more" of myself each day to help me get through. I thought I was learning the lessons that God wanted me to see. But God was still not moving me from my job and allowing me to stay home.

Contentment means that my heart is satisfied in my situation, that I am not constantly looking for something more or greater. Was I really content in my situation? No! I complained that I had to go into work each day even though it gave us a lifestyle of ease when it came to finances. I selfishly just wanted to give it all up to make myself feel better in my parenthood. I didn't care what the ripple effect to my daughter or those around me would be. I didn't realize that leaving when I wanted to leave would cause more harm than good. But God obviously knew. He was trying to help me see that I needed to be content in the situations that He placed me in, that complaining about those situations is the same as complaining about Him because He allowed this to take place. And being content means a change of perspective, a change of heart. A change that takes over your whole being. A change that shows you are willing to walk through all that

God has in-store and do it with a smile on your face. Not a fake smile. A smile of pure joy and appreciation that God has given us the blessing of another day to live for Him. A smile of contentment.

> *I rejoiced greatly in the Lord that at last you renewed your concern for me. Indeed, you were concerned, but you had no opportunity to show it. I am not saying this because I am in need, for I have learned to be content whatever the circumstances. I know what it is to be in need, and I know what it is to have plenty. I have learned the secret of being content in any and every situation, whether well fed or hungry, whether living in plenty or in want. I can do all this through him who gives me strength.*
> Philippians 4:10-13 (NIV)

"I don't like it, but I will take it"

You have done everything the little ones have asked. You have fed them, played with them, given them all your attention, worked hard so they have the necessities, and they are still not grateful or fully understand what it means to serve others like you have done for them their entire lives. At the slightest possibility that one sibling would get the special silverware over the other, or dislike the meal you slaved away at the entire day, a fit ensues when said child doesn't like the outcome. You lovingly let your child watch a movie and when they don't get to watch a second movie they scream and flail and throw a fit. You teach your children to be grateful and kind and appreciate all that God has blessed them with and remind them constantly that there are other children who are starving, so eat your pasta with red sauce! But to no avail, there is always a fight that comes when said child doesn't get their way. I don't teach them to be ungrateful. I don't teach them to be selfish and greedy. I don't let them watch anything or read anything to them other than biblical principles, wholesome and pure. To be honest, I don't really let my kids into society! I shelter and guard their innocence every chance I get. But they still act that way because they are sinful little humans, but so are we all.

We have a phrase in my family that we have been teaching our children. Instead of getting angry all the time when they don't get their way, we tell them a better response would be, "I don't like it, but I will take it!" Now this, to no surprise, doesn't always work, but my prayer is that they will start to understand the meaning behind it. Life doesn't always go our way, in fact many times it's the complete opposite of our way. But we need to learn that even if we don't like the answer, the outcome, the story, it is a tremendous blessing to just have another breath to breathe.

I will take whatever I am given while I live here on earth because one day it will all end. Do I want to fully live the life that God has blessed me with, or do I want to throw it all away? Am I willing to say this to my heavenly Father, "I don't like it God, but I will take it!" I will take everything that is given to me whether it be good or bad. In the good we see the blessing. In the bad we *find* the good. I will bear all that you ask of me in the knowledge that one day there will be no more suffering. No pain. No disappointment. As my four-year-old daughter said to me the other day, "Jesus didn't want to die mommy, but He did because God asked Him to, and He loves us." Are we willing to do the same for the One who asks so much less of us? Who asks us only to love Him and follow Him and work at building our relationship with Him?

Not only was I not content with my situation my husband was not content in his. He was a stay-at-home dad and while he loved the time with his little girl, he had a hard time adjusting to being home permanently. He hated that I had to go to work each day, knowing that I didn't want to be there, and knowing that he couldn't do anything about it. The days were just as stressful for him as they were me and add to that the fact, he had just been in a serious car accident that affected his brain in a severe way. He wanted my job, and I wanted his job and both of us would have done anything to be in the other person's shoes.

After seven months of my husband searching for a job and trying to get even one callback nothing presented itself. Our daughter was almost two now and I started to enjoy work and tried to be content each day I went. I focused on how I could bless and serve others which made the days more enjoyable. My husband was in a routine now and our daughter was getting older, so his days became less stressful and more fun. So, at this point we were both still not sure why or even if God would move us and switch our positions. Well, there was one more lesson that God needed me to absorb.

By the age of twenty-six I was making more money than I believed I would ever make in my life, but with that came a huge sense of security and identity. Even though the job was taking so much from me, I thought that I had done the right thing, gone to college, got a good job that pays well in my field of study, and climbed the ladder of success. That's the mindset that I grew up to understand. So as much as I wanted to be home with my child, I didn't want to leave the security of what my job meant, and I didn't want to leave the persona that I had built and the accolades and praise that went along with that. Being a stay-at-home mom is much less appealing in the world we live in today. I wanted to continue to feel the worth that came with my prestigious job and was scared about the hole that job would leave when it was gone.

> But Godliness with contentment is great gain. For we brought nothing into the world, and we can take nothing out of it. But if we have food and clothing, we will be content with that. Those who want to get rich fall into temptation and a trap and into many foolish and harmful desires that plunge people into ruin and destruction. For the love of money is a root of all kinds of evil. Some people, eager for money, have wandered from faith and pierced themselves with many griefs.
>
> 1 Timothy 6:6-10 (NIV)

I hadn't realized how much I allowed money and status to wrap me up like a blanket and keep me safe and warm. The name I had built in my career was filling up my emotional cup. The praise, accomplishments, and power that the job brought were my world, were what kept me going. I realized that I had to get away from this dangerous world. I realized that I needed to build my identity in someone else. That it wasn't about me and my job. At the end of the day, I was still just another worker with a paycheck, to be replaced at any time. The company was fine before I got there and would be fine long after I'm gone. This job was where I found my worth, but not for much longer.

As the months went by with no prospective jobs for my husband, I felt the Lord calling me to leave my job, sight unseen. For the longest time I had made the excuse that I couldn't leave my job because we were talking about having baby number two and we needed the health care that my job brought. I knew deep down that there was a more pressing reason to leave. God wanted me to step out in the grandest leap of faith I had ever made. Without my husband having a job, and no idea where or how we would pay for our very expensive personal health care, I walked into my boss's office, my knees shaking with nervousness, and told him that after my last main project, in three months, I would be leaving. The instant that I told my boss I was leaving I felt the greatest release from within. I felt as though I was riding on cloud nine, floating right up to Heaven.

The very next day when I returned home from work my husband had told me that he had gotten a call from a company wanting him to come in for an interview! Over seven months of silence, to a phone interview in one day. The one day that I jumped over the edge and fell into God's arms of grace and peace. By the end of that week, my husband would have a full-time job with better health care than my current job and I would be on my way to being a full time stay-at-home mom! God is good all the time!

When my first day to be a stay-at-home mom came, I was extremely nervous. I had no confidence at all. This was due largely to the fact that because Ben was off and with me ALL the time I was never alone and had never really taken care of my child solo. On day two of my new job my daughter and I were playing and as she went to run away, I grabbed her arm and it dislocated at the elbow! I was horrified! I didn't know what to do, I was panicking, sobbing. I called my husband right away and started driving to the ER as fast as I could! I couldn't believe that on my second day this was happening. It wasn't a good start to my already zero confident mindset.

It would take months for me to fully embrace this new lifestyle, this much slower pace of life! But it was still hard to not feel worthless when I was harvesting so much worth at my previous job. Those who stay home with their children know how much of a thankless job that it is. Being at home made me feel empty, incomplete. I didn't really know how else to feel. My sense of purpose was at an all-time low. I lost who I was, what I liked or disliked; I was aimless when those five minutes came that I had to myself. At times I lost all aspects of me, who I was, and what I was doing in this life.

The triggers in my past taught me that where I found my worth, identity, and purpose was normal; it came from my job, the next activity coming up, the things this world had to offer. But all this really needs to come from God! Intuitively we know this, but it is really hard to shift our mindset after years of a bad habit.

Stasi Eldridge, in her book *Becoming Myself*, talks about worth as being passed down to us from our mothers or withheld by them whether they realize it or not. "A mother cannot pass on what she does not possess. And neither can we. Mothers have the ability to withhold acceptance, value, love… Or based our self-worth on anything other than the fact that we exist. God does not do that. Our worth is not based on what we do, which life path we choose, or what we believe. Our worth is inherent in the fact that we are image bearers of the living God. Our worth is based on the fact that we are alive. We are human beings. Our worth is immeasurable. Our worth as a woman does not come to us when we believe in Jesus Christ as our Savior. It comes in our creation."[15]

My worth, my purpose, my identity.

All of these aspects come from God solely because I exist.

I was created in the image of God.

There is no badge for good works that makes me worthy in God's eyes.

There is no job, or child, or hobby that can fill the purpose in my life. My purpose is to live each day for God, sharing the good news with those all around me, and showing the love of Christ to those who may never see it from anyone else in this sinful world.

There is nothing on this earth that can build my identity and not leave me feeling empty and disappointed. Building my identity in the objects of this world will fail me every time. My identity comes from Christ alone. He will never fail me. He will never disappointment me. He will never leave me. He will never stop loving me and pursuing me. He will never stop loving and pursuing you!

When I realized this, when I let God fully immerse me in this truth, my attitude and heart began to change. I no longer felt the weight of staying home with my children. I marveled at the way God had orchestrated our paths. I soaked in the little details about my children that only I could know by watching them grow each day, the nuances that made their character and personality so special. I could see God shaping their hearts and relished in the moments when they emotionally prayed or talked about God. I embraced the role that God had always chosen for me. I fell in love with this new position and my new tiny bosses! I fell on my knees and thanked God for this tremendous blessing!

If Jesus had Facebook

I am not a social media wiz to say the least. I have one social media app, Facebook, that I got in college and only kept it to keep in touch with those that would be heading back to their hometowns after graduation. I am not on Twitter, Instagram, TikTok, Snapchat, you name it, I don't have it. But I do like my Facebook. There is comfort in scrolling on the home page looking to see what other people are up to, in a very non-creepy way. There is a mind numbing, get my brain out of the current situation and onto someone else's life feeling, especially being a stay-at-home mom. Facebook is my numbing out time. All bad, I totally understand, but all human.

One day, when I was on Facebook and I was longing to be in someone else's seemingly picture-perfect event or life I got to thinking about Jesus and what it would be like if He had Facebook. Would I be scrolling through His pictures and checking His status to see where He went last or where He will be going next? Would I be checking to see who His friends are and long to be their friends? Would I friend request Jesus Himself and anxiously await His reply? Would I be so eager to get a Facebook message from Him or see how many times He liked one of my photos or status'? Would I even care at all, or would I scroll right past? Where do my priorities, my affections, my time, my energy, my whole heart lie? If the answer to most of these questions, true and honest answers, are no, then we need to take a better look at what is most important in our lives. Are we living in the world, just passing through until we reach our true home? Or are we living of the world, our hearts consumed with the pleasures that this world has to offer? Do we long to have a relationship with Jesus, a friendship, or are we just hoping we get to Heaven?

Do we see Jesus as the celebrity that we long to meet? And yes, that means we would long to meet Jesus in Heaven. We would have to give up this life that we may think is so wonderful and perfect and finally go home. A good friend of mine, Jaime, a pastor at our home church, preached a sermon entitled "A Foreigner's Vision." He said that our goal in life is a destination but that the destination is not a place, it's a Person! Why do we fight so hard to fit in when Jesus calls us to stand out amongst the crowd? We are foreigners to this world after all.[16]

Are we living life in this place trying to do as many good works as possible, believing that will get us into Heaven? Or are we actually living for Christ, in relationship with Christ, leaving each day better than the one before, leaving an image of Christ for all to see? Do we long to touch the very tip of the cloak of Jesus? Or do we watch as He passes us by?

> *"Since, then, you have been raised with Christ, set your hearts on things above, where Christ is, seated at the right hand of God. Set your minds on things above, not on earthly things. For you died, and your life is now hidden with Christ in God. When Christ, who is your life, appears, then you also will appear with Him in glory."*
> Colossians 3:1-4 (NIV)

> *"And wherever He went—into villages, towns or countryside—they placed the sick in the marketplaces. They begged Him to let them touch even the edge of His cloak, and all who touched it were healed."*
> Mark 6:56 (NIV)

Wrapped Up

Reflection Questions:

- Are there areas of your life where you need to say, "I don't like it God, but I will take it?"

- Is contentment a feeling or a choice?

- Closely examine how you spend your time each day. What insignificant things are you choosing to invest your time in over cultivating a relationship with Christ? How do you feel when someone else is chosen over you? How do you suppose Jesus feels when we choose "Facebook" over Him?

- Are you living in the waiting?

- Where do you find your worth?

"Therefore we do not lose heart. Though outwardly we are wasting away, yet inwardly we are being renewed day by day. For our light and momentary troubles are achieving for us an eternal glory that far outweighs them all. So we fix our eyes not on what is seen, but on what is unseen, since what is seen is temporary, but what is unseen is eternal."

2 Corinthians 4:16-18 (NIV)

Chapter 7

RECKLESS LOVE

It was a cold March evening. The first of many snowflakes fell from the sky and melted on my perfectly styled hair. I was wearing a thin coat, obviously not expecting to be standing outside for this long. I was freezing as I stood there jumping up and down to keep warm. The snow piling up on the sidewalk as the line we were standing in crept forward ever so slowly. Those around us trying to figure out if they were in the correct line or if they could somehow make it to the front faster and into the warm building that awaited.

For King & Country has been my favorite band since the beginning of their time. Despite this, I had never seen them in concert or even attended a concert in years. On this very cold and snowy March night my husband had surprised me with tickets to what was known as the *Roadshow* concert in our hometown of Hershey, PA. This concert not only included my favorite band of all time, but a host of other Christian bands that I had come to adore. I was going to see these incredible bands and I would be doing it from my seat located on the floor, only a couple rows back from the stage! I had never had floor seats in my life! A close view of the stage and the ability to stand and worship without feeling like I was standing in the way of the person behind me (I am nearly six feet three inches). This is what awaited us if we could only get out of the insanely cold snow and to our seats before the show started, preferably before the snow totally ruined my "not made for being wet" hair. That turned out to be the least of our worries that night.

Because our seats were on the floor, our tickets were a special VIP pass. Unfortunately, that didn't really mean much as we came to find out that almost all the tickets had that printed on them and we didn't get into the arena any faster than anyone else did. After what seemed like a lifetime of standing in this line and now not able to feel my toes from my not so warm, but super cute boots, we were at the door and getting our tickets scanned to go inside!

The lights were dimmed as we entered the front of the arena. We made our way past the Compassion and merchandise stands in which I saw a very sharp looking *for King & Country* green bomber jacket. My husband and I decided to grab a little snack and take our seats and then maybe do some shopping before the show started. I was very hungry and usually required a snack every so often; I was, after all, pregnant with our second child!

The day before I had gone to the hospital to have a checkup for my baby. All went pretty well, only there seemed to be a concern about some bleeding I had. Unusual for me and a little scary as I had not had this problem during my first pregnancy, but after a few tests the doctor said that there was nothing to worry about and that I could keep on doing life normally. That for me meant the concert of my dreams!

After having a little snack, I excitedly went to the merchandise table and purchased myself the green *for King & Country* jacket and wore it back to my seat. Shortly after, the lights went down, and the music started to play. *Bethel* was the opening act and as the vibes started to pick up, we were all on our feet with expectancy. The music hit me and sent a vibration through my entire body shaking the core of my soul. Only, the minute that I stood up, during the first song of this dream concert, a warmth rushed through my body. I had a feeling as though my water had broken, and the baby was coming! But this couldn't be as I was only nine weeks into the pregnancy. I immediately knew that something was very wrong and made my way to the restroom, although I had a pretty good idea of what was happening.

Inside the stall of the bathroom, with no phone and no way to get in contact with my husband, as I ran away so fast, I barely had time to tell him where I was going, I sobbed as I took in the realty of my situation. I was alone. Instead of water, I found blood. I was bleeding out. I was unsure if this meant that I was losing my precious baby. I could barely hold myself together. I was frightened for the baby's life and for my own. I wanted my husband to be right beside me, but of course he didn't even know what was going on. I could barely breathe until God filled me with life once again. In the moments I was running into the bathroom and taking in the situation the second song by *Bethel* started to play. It was my favorite song by them, *Reckless Love*. The most perfect song that could have played in the exact time of my need.

I sat in the stall and listened to these words from God and prayed. I prayed that God would show me all He had for me. That I would not let fear dominate this situation and potentially make things worse, if that was even possible. That I would have a perspective of seeing the good in this traumatic event. That I wouldn't fall back into Satan's trap like I had so many times before.

This time, this story, this event was different from all the rest in my life. For the first time I went straight to God and didn't turn back, didn't question, wasn't angry, nothing. Total unending peace. My baby could've been dying, but that was out of my control. The whole situation was out of my control and I handed everything over to God; the events that had taken place in the past four years had geared me for this moment. I had finally learned to kneel, thank God for everything He had given me, and wholeheartedly trust God and His plans.

As the song continued to play and I got situated well enough to head out to find my husband God had sent him to me. He was standing right outside the ladies' bathroom waiting. I told him we needed to head to the hospital right away and find out if the baby was gone. And just like that we left. We left the amazing seats. We left the insane worship. We left the dream concert. We left to God's reckless love.

We headed to the car and realized it had snowed several inches by now and driving the five miles to the hospital would take some time, plus we had to clean off the car, so we didn't get into a car accident as well. Remember, we had already been through that and I didn't really want to relive those times. The short distance to the ER took an eternity in the unplowed roads ahead of us, but when we did finally arrive, I calmly walked into the ER and told them what happened. They did a bunch of tests and I saw lots of doctors and then had to wait, again. Wait for an answer of whether my baby was alive or had met Jesus.

And in total honesty, instead of feeling angry with God or crippled with heartache over what answer we were waiting for, I felt nothing but calm and peace. I knew that this was out of my control. I knew that I had done nothing wrong. I felt no shame or guilt or anger or anything. Only peace. This, my friends, is not easy to say or feel. It's not an overnight feeling that you can get to by wishing for. This is something that God had been molding in my life. This was a few years journey worth of heartache and anger and shame and guilt and you name it. It was years of prayer! All leading to this moment and any other moments to come in our broken world. This was part of my sanctification process.

In the waiting, through the attitude and perspective that I brought to this horrific situation I got to witness to all those I came in contact with at that hospital. Ben and I got to share our story of the last few years and share what we should have been doing instead of sitting in this room waiting for our test results. We could show these people the spirit of the Lord living inside of us with our graciousness to them. We got to share the good news of the gospel of Jesus Christ. We got to show them that Jesus calls us to be different and explain why our attitudes seem not of this world, not what they have seen in many.

Being fearful would do nothing. Being worried would be even worse. As I was getting another ultrasound done the technician anxiously searched for a heartbeat, I looked away leaving God to take control and show trust in Him. After a few seconds of searching, a heartbeat was found! And as I looked up at the screen the technician started showing us the entirety of our precious little one! And miraculously the technician couldn't find anything wrong with our baby!

Even more miraculously I didn't feel surprised by this answer. Somehow, I felt as though, through His overwhelming peace, God had already given me the answer before this moment.

The doctor who looked over all my results continued to explain the findings of why I ended up there in the first place. There was apparently a sack of blood in with the baby, but not attached to the baby, that was most likely the result of a failed attempt at my body creating a second baby and the reason for my trip to the ER. I was told to monitor my activity and any unusual signs with my body. And then the doctor said that our baby had a 50/50 chance of survival. I was heartbroken by the news that my baby may not make it to birth.

I honestly thought that miscarriages were very rare in the times that we lived in, but recently there were several women that I know who had one. When I heard the heartbeat on the ultrasound, I was relieved and wasn't expecting the doctor to tell me that this precious life I was carrying still only had a 50/50 chance of survival. But, as devastated as I was that in a couple months, I may not be holding a sweet baby in my hands, I knew that this was out of my control. I knew God had a plan for us all in this moment and it was attitude and outlook that God wanted to see. He wanted to see if I would give up or hold onto trust and faith in Him. I knew that all I could do in this moment was thank the Lord for His hand of protection around my little one *this* night and live each day to come thankful for His blessings.

At forty-one weeks, on the night that I was attending my brother-in-law's wedding rehearsal, nearly one hour away from my hospital, our little boy (a strong fighter) entered the world. He arrived thirty minutes after entering the same ER that we had gone to on that dreary March night.

Because it took us so long to get to the hospital, and with our little guy coming so quickly after we had arrived, I wasn't able to get an epidural. Although my birth plan this time around was to hold out as long as I could and not get the epidural or any medical assistance. My best friend had told me that on her baby number two she opted out of the medication and it was the best thing she had ever done. So, in taking her advice, and also kind of forced into it, I opted for no epidural and I have to say it was the smartest decision that I made. I felt like a champion afterward, getting right out of the bed and walking myself to the bathroom minutes after giving birth. I was a little nervous that I would have postpartum like I did when I had my daughter, but God redeems! I never had postpartum the second time around, in fact I had felt better than I could have ever imagined! A completely different mom than I was three years earlier. A more confident mom. A more confident woman. A more confident daughter of God.

When our daughter was born, we wanted to pick a very special name, a unique and uncommon name, one that reflected all that God had done in the months leading up to her arrival. We named her Tobyn, which means God is good. And God is certainly good all the time, especially in our lives the year that she was born. So naturally, when it came time to choose our son's name, we wanted the same thing because God was still working in our lives and showing us some miraculous and amazing things about Him and ourselves. We named our son Ellis, a form of Elijah, which means the Lord is my God, a reminder to us that the Lord is in control of everything, is over everything, that there is no other god than my God! Elijah did some great things in the Old Testament and we pray that our little man does great things for the Lord.

You know, throughout these many years of struggle, wrestling with the Lord and battling spiritual warfare, in some ways I felt like Job. Now let me make it clear, my life will probably never be as difficult as Job's, but the struggle is real. Job lost literally everything in one day. I may have had hard times, but I did not lose anyone in my life and at times throughout our suffering God has blessed us in tremendous ways. But what I learned from Job's story is that he was handpicked by God. Just like we are handpicked by God to walk in our stories. The stories that God has given us. The stories that couldn't be walked by any other nor could we walk in anyone else's. And you know what I learned through all this? It is an honor to be handpicked by God! Let me be clear when I say in the midst of the trials, suffering, and heartache this concept is not the first thing that comes to us. We essentially believe that being handpicked by God is the most glorious thing until God handpicks us to carry out something much harder than we anticipated. But I believe that if what God chooses me for can bring one more life, one more hurting and desperate soul, to the feet of the Father, then I will gladly go through the pain again.

Let's take a closer look at the bittersweet story of Job:

Job was a prominent man in the land of Uz, blameless and upright. He had status, a strong family, livestock, land, and servants. He made sacrifices to the Lord each morning for his entire family. "Then the Lord said to Satan, 'Have you considered my servant Job? There is no one on earth like him; he is blameless and upright, a man who fears God and shuns evil.' 'Does Job fear God for nothing?' Satan replied. 'Have you not put a hedge around him and his household and everything he has? You have blessed the work of his hands, so that his flocks and herds are spread throughout the land. But now stretch out your hand and strike everything he has, and he will surely curse you to your face.' The Lord said to Satan, 'Very well, then, everything he has is in your power, but on the man himself do not lay a finger'" (Job 1:8-12, NIV).

Right here God chooses Job to carry out His mission. Job, a man who seemingly had everything and was a righteous man. What better example to use than Job? Satan thought that he could trip God up as if God made a mistake in handpicking Job, that Job only faithfully followed God because of how blessed he was. Take that away and Satan was sure that Job would forsake God.

God didn't make a mistake. Satan didn't ask for God to choose someone that he could go after. God offered Job up as a sacrifice because He knew that Job would be able to handle it. He knew that Job was up to the task. He knew that Job would not deny Him. He knew that Job could walk through the fire, and even though he may be altered by the heat, Job would not be consumed by the flames. In John 15:16 (NIV), Jesus says this: "You did not choose me, *but I chose you and appointed you so that you might go and bear fruit*—fruit that will last—and so that whatever you ask in my name the Father will give you." Each one of us is handpicked to be written into God's story for better or for worse. God has already won the war and we should be so honored to fight alongside Him!

In an instant, Job's world was turned upside down. He received "that" message that no one ever believes will come. Job lost his livestock, his servants, and his children, all in the same day! And do you know what he did when he was informed of these things? He fell on his knees in worship! "The Lord gave and the Lord has taken away; may the name of the Lord be praised. In all this, Job did not sin by charging God with wrongdoing" (Job 1:21b-22a, NIV).

Then, after the Lord had talked to Satan again about Job, Job was troubled with painful sores. Job's own wife told him to give up, curse God, and die. To which Job replied, "Shall we accept good from God, and not trouble?" (Job 2:10b, NIV). But then a shift in perspective comes from Job, a human perspective. He questions God and starts to ask WHY. Why is this happening to me? He curses the day of his birth and believes that he has no peace on this earth, only turmoil. Job's friends come and try to convince Job that God would not be doing this to him if he hadn't done something wrong.

I have been here in this moment feeling like Job, and I'm sure if you've read this far you have been there too. I once believed that the only way to have peace or live peacefully is when I am comfortable and when God tidied up the mess that was and is my life. We can have comfortable lives and wrestle with our enemies within, never having true peace. I wasn't comfortable when my husband was almost killed in a car accident, but God brought me peace. I wasn't comfortable when I believed the lies that I was destroying the relationship with my daughter in my severe postpartum depression, but God brought me peace. I wasn't comfortable with a career life change from a high profile and prominent job to being a selfless stay-at-home mom, but God brought me peace. I wasn't comfortable as I was being rushed to the hospital with the feeling of losing my unborn child, but God brought me peace. Get the picture? *Peace does not necessarily equal my comfort, but through the peace that only God can give we can have comfort in our souls.*

By the end of the book, Job asks God to come and explain to him why this is happening. But instead of God answering the question, God points Job to all that the Lord has accomplished, the universe in all its splendor. To show

Job that He has created all things and in so doing has control over all things. To remind Job that in all that was happening in his life Satan was doing the afflicting and God was performing the restoration! Whether or not we can wrap our minds around why God is doing something is irrelevant. See, the point is not the why. The point is submission, awe, trust, obedience, and the list can go on. To humbly submit to the all-powerful One who created the universe and everything in it. Awe of the beauty that the Lord has made in the midst of our suffering and trials. Trust that God is in control all the time, not just when times are best. Obedience to walk through ALL that God has in store for us and be honored through it.

"The book of Job teaches us that it is futile to try to understand the reason behind our suffering. It is enough to know that God is in control and that He is our refuge and strength in times of trouble. Like Job, we also need to learn that God is not bound by our understanding or by our lack of it. He is free and subject to no will but His own. He does not owe us an explanation for His actions."[17]

In the end God restores. Though Job in his humanity may have questioned, his faith remained. Job didn't just follow the Lord because it was convenient, in fact it was very inconvenient, as his strong faith was the reason God chose him. God rewarded that faith in the restoration of double all that was lost. But more importantly than that, God restores our hearts. He strips down all that Satan has covered us in, the dirt, debris, filth, and shines us up like a new penny. God molds us in our pursuit of holiness!

Wrapped Up

Reflection Questions:

- What areas of your life do you feel that you have control over? Do you cause your wounds to heal? Do you keep your heart beating? Do you keep the oncoming truck in its lane?

- How much time and energy do we as humans spend attempting to gain more control over our lives? Have we been successful?

- Does knowing that we are in control of very little in life bring you peace or anxiety? How would your life change if you submitted what you don't control to God's provision?

- In what capacity do you relate to Job? What parts of his story bring conviction?

- What is the posture of your heart when trials come? Do you plead injustice? Does it validate your anger? Do you respond with humility, thankfulness, and worship?

"Surely God is my salvation; I will trust and not be afraid. The Lord, the Lord Himself, is my strength and my defense; He has become my salvation. With joy you will draw water from the wells of salvation."
Isaiah 12:2-3 (NIV)

Chapter 8

A NEW WORLD

When I was in high school biology class, I remember near the end of the school year we watched a movie about a virus; very rare to watch movies in school, I'm with you, but a movie none-the-less. The premise was a monkey, carrying a deadly virus, infects a California town and very rapidly starts to spread through the air from person to person. As the lead doctor tries to find the source and a cure, the Army quarantines the entire town; no one in, no one out, and no family unit conversing with another. Sounds like unrealistic scary stuff I know, but in just a few years after this moment in high school I, along with the rest of the world, would get to somewhat experience this crisis.

There have been many movies recently depicting a dystopian, apocalyptic near future in which a virus or some other calamity decimates the human race and only a small handful of us are left. Many of these movies are about zombies, but you get the gist. Little did we all know that in the year 2020 the world that we all live in would become a version of this cinematic scenario, minus the zombies of course, and the world that we all knew would be gone forever.

In March of 2020 a viral pandemic swept across the globe bringing fear and panic through the hearts and souls of many, including me. I will admit to you that at first our family was very cautious about what was going on around us. We have faith in Christ and He gave me peace about this situation by not letting the fear of our family getting this virus consume me. With all the unknowns in what the media was saying, what doctors were saying, and what those around us were saying we played it safe and stayed home for about four weeks.

In this current crisis of our world, our government issued a decree of "social distancing" or "quarantine," telling the people to not leave their property, total lockdown. Schools across the country were shutdown, social events and concerts canceled, all the major sports teams modified their season or even canceled them entirely, businesses were told that unless they were deemed "essential" they had to close their doors and forfeit their means to take care of those around them. But worst of all, most church doors were closed and events canceled. The world as we once knew had been completely shut down in the matter of twenty-four hours. This scenario would continue for months.

The biggest thing for me to come out of all of this was that all shall wear a mask when going out into society, a mandate from our government for the health and safety of others, not ourselves. Most businesses would not allow you to enter their store without a mask on. I wrestled with the decision of what I should do. I didn't want to wear the mask. I wasn't fearful about the virus at all. I knew I wasn't contagious because our whole family didn't leave our house in four weeks and therefore wouldn't harm anyone else that I came across. There wasn't one ounce of my being that made me believe that a mask was needed. I felt like it was a false sense of security for everyone and everyone was buying into the lie that was being forced upon us. I was told many times that if I didn't wear a mask that I didn't love people. But I wondered why that had to be the only answer. I in no way wasn't wanting to wear a mask because I didn't love people, a mask honestly gave me anxiety.

I hate seeing people wearing masks all around me, I have always hated that since I was a young girl. It was always a marker of distrust for me because you couldn't see their true face and somehow seeing their true face showed me their true self. It was also a symbol throughout my life of someone bad, a robber, or thief, or kidnapper. Someone who wanted to deceive by disguising their face. I couldn't get past all the shame that I felt wearing a mask and becoming the stereotype that a mask represented. I couldn't get past the shame of not wearing a mask and the vision of hate for others that that stereotype brought. I was lost in the middle of this not so black and white storyline not able to make a clear decision and unable to clearly hear God's voice through the shame I felt on the inside. It took a lot of conversations with other believers and even more soul searching with the Lord for me to lay down my reservations.

I ended up choosing to wear the mask out of respect for those that the Lord had put into our roles of leadership, to show respect to those around me, and to set a good example for my children and headed out to the store. As I walked through the store people didn't even want to look at me and frankly you didn't want to look at them. My heart ached that no one could see me give them a friendly smile and they couldn't hear the encouraging words of love I would try to send their way. When I got back to my car after I had finished shopping, I sat there for about twenty minutes with tears streaming down my face. A wave of emotion had come surging up to the surface.

Until this time, I really didn't have any emotion about the virus. I wasn't scared. I didn't know anyone who had the virus. I was a stay-at-home mom with kids who aren't old enough to attend school so there were no school closures or homeschooling. My husband was still working, but now got to work from home so that was almost a bonus for me. My life was honestly not that much different than before except for not being able to take my kids to certain activities and places like the grocery store (as at least one of them was sure to lick a cart handle the minute I strapped them in). But this first time going out into the new world we now lived in was different.

It was sad.

It was darker.

It was lonely.

I was out in society, but not really. There was no community, people even avoided each other. There were no relationships. It was a lonely place. I had relished in the fact that I got to leave the house kid free and go into society for some relaxation, even if just to the grocery store, and seconds after I entered the store I wanted to leave. It was a heartbreaking experience. I was heartbroken at the realization that our world was not the same and may never be the same again. I wondered if this was really what our Father wants. This disconnect and loneliness even when we are in society with others. Will life ever be the same when this is all over?

As the world spiraled out of control in one way after another, I clawed to grab control of anything I could. I studied up on all things pandemic and read countless articles that of course fit my belief in the current scenario. See, I had already painted a picture in my head about what this world looked like and walking around wearing a mask all the time was not in that picture. A mask was painted in another's picture, not mine. The more knowledge I acquired the more powerful I thought I had become in all things control. The knowledge I gained was another brick I used to put up my wall and I got my defenses ready when anyone came to knock it down.

I was afraid of the change. The so-called "new normal" that was constantly talked about. I guess if I am really being honest, I was afraid that my freedom was being taken away. Having freedom in our country can become an idol, especially when you see the slightest change in having it taken away, but in reality, my freedom was being taken away not by the government but by Satan and myself. By constantly getting involved with what was going on and pouring myself into the knowledge that I had come to behold I was taking away my own freedom by consuming myself with the world. But the mistake that I made was where I was getting my knowledge from. The only knowledge I should have been gaining was from Christ, through His personal words in the Bible, NOT from the latest news article.

Essentially, in our world we were seeing a division of one side verses another. It didn't matter what the one side or the other stood for, it could have been anything. But like the parting of the Red Sea our world split down the middle and we were all being forced to choose. See what was happening in our world was a lack of faith in God and frankly a lack of God in our world. It wasn't people choosing one side over the other; it was Satan through those people destroying everything good that God had made. "For our struggle is not against flesh and blood, but against the rulers, against the authorities, against the powers of this dark world and against the spiritual forces of evil in the heavenly realms" (Ephesians 6:12, NIV).

We are allowing those in this world to persuade our thoughts into thinking one way or the other. We are allowing Satan himself to justify why we believe something, and we are not reaching out to the only One who can save us! We are doing Satan's dirty work for him. Satan watches as we tear ourselves apart while he slithers past undetected. We are fighting the WRONG enemy! We should be standing together, as children of the Lord made in His image, in God's army fighting the true enemy, Satan!

When I look at the way the world has been this past year, it seems as though the second coming has got to be right around the corner. With all the tragedies and chaos spoken about the signs of the end times you wonder if Jesus is going to come back tomorrow, but we have to remember that Jesus knew that this was coming and warned His disciples. "When you hear of wars and rumors of wars, do not be alarmed. Such things must happen, but the end is still to come. Nation will rise against nation, and kingdom against kingdom. There will be earthquakes in various places, and famines. These are the beginning of birth pains" (Mark 13:7-8, NIV).

Satan is still using the same old tricks to deceive humans that he did in the garden of Eden. He is still stealing the hearts of those around us and we need to take action.

We need to fight for our God and battle against evil. We need to pray for those around us and not criticize their every move because it is a different view than ours. We need to pray for the hurting and lost souls who need the message of Jesus Christ, our Savior. We need to not be so quick to judge others when we cannot know the full story behind anyone but ourselves. We need to ask God for wisdom to do what He would have us do in this new world around us. Dear ones, this message is as much for you as it is for me!

With all that has happened, we will never be able to go back. We will never have the world we once knew. We have been kicked out of our Eden and sent wandering into a new world. My prayer for us all is that this new world is seen as a new opportunity. To realize that we don't need half the things we once had or were able to do. That the ones whom God chose for us to do life with are all we need. That we can slow down and focus our attention not on the endless sports activities or running around, but on Him. That we can brush off the dirt and debris sitting on top of our Bibles, and our hearts, and dig into God's Word allowing it to be the only thing to fill us up.

My prayer is that we learn to love. Not just loving those who love us, that is easy. Are we willing to love those who are hard to love? Love those that are different from us who have different opinions. Love those who have hurt us or wronged us in some way. Love despite any and all circumstances. Love as Christ shows us every second of every day. The love He showed us when He died for us; the love for all sinners. "I thank Christ Jesus our Lord, who has given me strength, that He considered me trustworthy, appointing me to His service. Even though I was once a blasphemer and a persecutor and a violent man, I was shown mercy because I acted in ignorance and unbelief. *The grace of our Lord was poured out on me abundantly, along with the faith and love that are in Christ Jesus.* Here is a trustworthy saying that deserves full acceptance: *Christ Jesus came into the world to save sinners—of whom I am the worst*" (1 Timothy 1:12-15, NIV).

Our children depend on this.

Our relationships depend on this.

Our lives depend on this.

Our country depends on this.

Our world this side of Heaven depends on this.

So, go out into the world and spread the love of Christ! "Love is patient, love is kind. It does not envy, it does not boast, it is not proud. It does not dishonor others, it is not self-seeking, it is not easily angered, it keeps no record of wrongs. Love does not delight in evil but rejoices with the truth. It always protects, always trusts, always hopes, always perseveres. Love never fails... And now these three remain: faith, hope and love. But the greatest of these is love" (1 Corinthians 13:4-8a, 13, NIV).

Life is unpredictable.

Life is hard and messy.

One minute we are climbing the highest mountains, and the next minute we are crashing to the lowest point of the valley.

But we know this.

If we are being honest with ourselves, we know that life doesn't turn out the way that WE plan. We know that no matter how hard we try to control the outcome of our lives we will fail every time. So why, when life takes the unexpected twists and turns, do we complain and grumble and ask God those same old questions we asked at the beginning of this book?

I love the faith that Paul has in Acts 14 as he and Barnabas go into Lystra. After Paul healed a man who was lame, the Lycaonian people believed that Paul and Barnabas were gods who came down to them in human form (Acts 14:8-13, NIV). Paul tries to witness to the people telling them the good news of the living God, but the crowd would not listen.

"Then some Jews came from Antioch and Iconium and won the crowd over. *They stoned Paul and dragged him outside the city*, thinking he was dead. But after the disciples had gathered around him, *he got up and went back into the city.* The next day he and Barnabas left for Derbe" (Acts 14:19-20, NIV).

Now, I don't know about you but if I was just stoned to near death my first reaction would NOT be to get up and go back into that same city. How much does Paul love God, have faith in God, and trust that God has a plan for his life? Would I be willing to do this?

"'We must go through many hardships to enter the kingdom of God,' they said" (Acts 14:22b, NIV). Just like Job God spared Paul's life BUT not the misery of the stoning. They kept their lives but suffered tremendous hardships throughout those lives. When the storm beats us down and leaves us with bloody wounds to near death, are we willing to get back up and head right back into that storm? Will we have the faith and confidence to face the same enemy that just ripped us apart? Will we follow the example of Paul and many others in the Bible to help pull us back when we go astray?

Will we love?

Will we fight against evil?

Will we persevere through our storms?

Will we look up to God for peace to boldly walk the treacherous terrain that is the rest of our lives?

Wrapped Up

Reflection Questions:

- Is there someone in your life that God is asking you to love who may be hard to love?

- How often do you pray for your enemies, or those you don't like? (Matthew 5:44) Would you consider committing to pray for those who you struggle to love?

- Do you struggle with change or embrace it? Are you longing for life to get back to "the way things were?" Why?

- Examine your heart, what areas of life are you attempting to gain control over? Have you been successful? Has this pursuit brought any peace?

- During your current circumstances, are you praying for God to remove you from your situation or pursuing how you can be used where you have been placed?

"I have told you these things, so that in me you
may have peace. In this world you will have trouble.
But take heart! I have overcome the world."
John 16:33 (NIV)

EPILOGUE

If I think about all the changes and struggles, we have faced
over the past five years, on the surface, from the outside
world looking in, it feels like one bad thing after another.
Like our faith has been tested in every way imaginable. Like
God never showed up. Like the storms will never end.

Even as I write this to you now, putting God's truth into
the hands of a soul who desperately needs to hear the words,
I know that evil is on the prowl. I know a storm may be
coming around the corner. God doesn't cause complications,
pain, struggle, hardship, death, destruction, in our lives, but
He does allow them. He allows it to remind us of His power
and mercy and grace. How the only real hope we have to get
through this life is to trust in His strength, because ours will
fail every time. Christ has not allowed me to walk through
anything that He has not already equipped me to bear.

Why do we believe that when we choose a life of following Christ that we will not suffer? I believed this lie. Jesus
Himself, in all of His sinless nature, suffered greatly on this
earth for you and for me. He paid the ultimate price! He
knows what we are suffering through because He has person-
ally felt it for Himself.

"Jesus was born into the toughest of conditions; he was misunderstood, mistreated, and rejected throughout his life. His closest friends forsook him when the going got tough. He was betrayed by those he should have been able to trust. He was regularly hungry and knew what it was like to be homeless. He felt the sting of the worst kind of injustice. He endured tortuous physical suffering. From birth, his life was never easy, and his death was marked by public shame. No one rose to his defense. He not only suffered; he suffered alone. Even his father turned his back on him in his deepest moment of agony. He did not use his power to make his life easy or to escape injustice and torture. He came to earth knowing what he would face, and he faced it all for us."[18]

God allows us the freedom to make choices. In times of darkness, we can choose to stand firm deeply rooted in truth, falling into the arms of Jesus or our knees can shudder like a baby deer, breaking under the pressure of all the pain, shame, hurt; allowing Satan to pull us ever so quietly into the deep. What will you choose? What will I choose? Will we choose to follow the one who sneaks around in the night, slyly scheming about when to pounce next or the One who boldly and confidently stands in the light and knocks on the front door.

Will we choose death, or will we choose life? When we choose life, when we choose to be deeply rooted in our relationship with Christ, when we choose the truth of God and His goodness, we will unlock a treasure chest filled with peace, love, grace, mercy, contentment, and joy. Through any situation, this dark and broken world may throw at us, we will have the only One necessary in our corner, fighting against evil for our hearts.

I used to pray for the Lord to make one thing easy in my life, just one thing. My prayers were very selfish and directed only at taking away the pain in the moment and not about asking the Lord for wisdom to open my eyes to what He was teaching me. "When you ask, you do not receive, because you ask with wrong motives, that you may spend what you get on your pleasures" (James 4:3, NIV).

If we are giving our whole hearts to Jesus, our lives will most likely be messy. They will be hard because we live in this broken, cruel, dark, and sinful world.

"If the world hates you, keep in mind that it hated me first. If you belonged to the world, it would love you as its own. As it is, you do not belong to the world, but I have chosen you out of the world. That is why the world hates you. Remember what I told you: 'A servant is not greater than his master.' If they persecuted me, they will persecute you also. If they obeyed my teaching, they will obey yours also… Whoever hates me hates my Father as well" (John 15:18-20, 23, NIV).

But here is where God offers the hope through all the suffering. Times are hard and dark, yes, in this life, this very short life. BUT God…but God offers the hope of Jesus Christ whom He sent to this earth to selflessly die for my sins, for your sins, only to rise again defeating all evil so that we may live with Him forever in Heaven.

I see how He used the gut wrenchingly hard times to humble me, grow me, and save me. He could not have done this without those times. I've seen how God has softened my dad's heart and brought him to Jesus. I've seen the miracles that God can perform. In the past few months, I have seen the love that a mother can give when they allow God to love on them, a restored bond that God has orchestrated through honesty and truth; the friend that I have longed to behold!

Now, I can say with confidence, that all that we have been through, all that we are going through, and all that is yet to come will always be worth it. The growth that I have experienced in my walk with Christ far outweighs any temporary loss or gain. If we aren't persecuted and evil isn't trying every way in the book to make our lives miserable and drag us down, what are we living for? How deep is our faith and trust in Jesus? It is God's glory that has become the most important to our family and my word it is GOOD!

Whether we believe it or not, God knits every moment we experience together to form His beautifully perfect tapestry known as our life. Each trial, tragedy, milestone is linked together. Moments that allow you to learn from one to the next, moments that you were chosen for to help someone else in need. Moments, that if we lay down ourselves and step out in our utmost vulnerability, can save the life of those closest to us. To save another soul.

My prayer is that this story, the one that God has written in my family's life will give you hope. I urge you to write your version of His story in your own life. If for nothing else as a reminder of God's goodness, faithfulness, and peace that He alone brought in your time of need. Because He *HAS* brought you goodness and faithfulness and peace. God *IS* goodness and faithfulness and peace. "Ask and it will be given to you; seek and you will find; knock and the door will be opened to you. For everyone who asks receives; the one who seeks finds; and to the one who knocks, the door will be opened" (Matthew 7:7-8, NIV). He never said that it would be easy, but He did promise peace and one day a forever home. A home in which you will be walking side by side with the Author and Creator of all things made new. A home God always intended for us here on earth. A home of eternal peace.

Until that time comes, I will wait with expectancy for the next storm that rolls my way knowing that somehow through the chaos and noise there is a lesson to be learned, a story to tell, and a life to be changed. And when the next time comes, I will hold out my arms and allow Christ to pull me back into His as He wraps me in His peace like He has done so many times before!

If you are looking for some key scripture verses, truths to hold onto in times of struggle about God's peace, here are a few more that kept me going:

> "The Lord gives strength to His people; the Lord blesses His people with peace" (Psalms 29:11, NIV).

> "I will listen to what God the Lord says; He promises peace to His people, His faithful servants—but let them not turn to folly" (Psalms 85:8, NIV).

> "Great peace have those who love your law, and nothing can make them stumble" (Psalms 119:165, NIV).

> "'Though the mountains be shaken and the hills be removed, yet my unfailing love for you will not be shaken nor my covenant of peace be removed', says the Lord, who has compassion on you" (Isaiah 54:10, NIV).

> "May the God of hope fill you with all joy and peace as you trust in Him, so that you may overflow with hope by the power of the Holy Spirit" (Romans 15:13, NIV).

ENDNOTES

1 Lysa Terkeurst, *It's Not Supposed To Be This Way* (Nashville: Nelson Books), 17.
2 Paul Tripp, "Women Helping Women, Session 2: Amazement vs. Faith," *Right Now Media*. Available at: https://www.rightnowmedia.org/Content/Series/742?episode=2.
3 C. S. Lewis, *The Screwtape Letters* (New York: HarperCollins Publishers, 1996), 151.
4 Charles Swindoll quote on attitude: https://www.goodreads.com/author/quotes/5139.Charles_R_Swindoll.
5 Stasi Eldredge, *Becoming Myself* (Colorado Springs: David C Cook), 254.
6 Priscilla Shirer, *Armor of God* (Nashville: LifeWay Press), 18, 20.
7 Priscilla Shirer, *Armor of God* (Nashville: LifeWay Press), 34.
8 Priscilla Shirer, "2019 Going Beyond Simulcast," *Lifeway Media*.
9 C.S. Lewis, *Mere Christianity* (New York: Simon & Schuster Touchstone edition, 1996), 109, 111.
10 Priscilla Shirer, *Armor of God* (Nashville: LifeWay Press), 61.
11 Paul Tripp, *Suffering* (Wheaton: Crossway), 164.
12 Priscilla Shirer, *Armor of God* (Nashville: LifeWay Press), 133.
13 Priscilla Shirer, *Armor of God* (Nashville: LifeWay Press), 98, 99.
14 Lysa Terkeurst, *Unglued* (Nashville: Nelson Books), 105.
15 Stasi Eldredge, *Becoming Myself* (Colorado Springs: David C Cook), 84.
16 Jaime Saez, "A Foreigners Vision," *Lebanon Area Evangelical Free Church*. September 29, 2019. Available at: http://www.lebefree.org/media-center/media-item/269/a-foreigners-vision.
17 George W. Knight and Rayburn W. Ray, *The Barbour Bible Reference Companion* (Uhrichsville: Barbour Books), 463.
18 Paul Tripp, *Suffering* (Wheaton: Crossway), 113.

2019 Family Photo—Tobyn, Lindsey, Ben, and Ellis
(Photo Credit: Inspired and Enchanted Photography)

9 781647 739034